Mostly

About Writing

Selected Essays of Nancy Martin

BOYNTON/COOK PUBLISHERS, INC.
UPPER MONTCLAIR, NEW JERSEY

HEINEMANN EDUCATIONAL BOOKS
LONDON

Library of Congress Cataloging in Publication Data

Martin, Nancy.
    Mostly about writing.
      1. Language arts—Addresses, essays,
lectures. 2. English language—Composition and
exercises—Addresses, essays, lectures. I. Title.
LB1576.M3794   1983   428'.007   83-9972
ISBN 0-86709-069-3

For information address Boynton/Cook Publishers, Inc., P.O. Box 860, 52 Upper
Montclair Plaza, Upper Montclair, NJ. 07043.

ISBN 0-86709-069-3

Printed in the United States of America

83 84 85 10 9 8 7 6 5 4 3 2 1

Published in Great Britain by Heinemann Educational Books Ltd. 22 Bedford
Square, London WC1B 3HH.
ISBN 0 435 10505 1

Preface

Some of the essays in this collection owe a great deal to other people. The essays in Section III, for instance, reflect some of the work done with the two projects, *The Development of Writing Abilities 11–18 Years* and *Writing Across the Curriculum 11–16 Years*. These two projects gave ten years of uninterrupted research and development; they involved hundreds of teachers and schools, and the outcomes have been influential in the USA as well as Britain. None of this could have happened without the funding by the Schools Council, and the generous support given by the London University Institute of Education in its sponsoring of the projects.

In this connection too I should like to acknowledge the great contribution that James Britton has made to my thinking—and indeed, to that of the whole project team. The lead he gave throughout the five years of the Writing Research powerfully influenced much of our subsequent thinking and procedures in the Writing Across the Curriculum study.

Finally, I want to thank my West Australian connection: Dr. Mossenson, Director General of Education, who gave me the opportunity to explore ways of evaluating work in schools, his colleagues in the Education Department, and colleagues in the English Department in the University of Western Australia where part of my work was located. It is impossible to do justice to what I gained from them, and from the many, many teachers who gave me the chance to make a large number of tapes and shared their ideas, their classrooms, and their students' writing so generously.

OTHER BOOKS OF SELECTED ESSAYS
AND TALKS IN THIS SERIES

ANN E. BERTHOFF
*The Making of Meaning: Metaphors, Models, and
Maxims for Writing Teachers*

JAMES BRITTON
Prospect and Retrospect: Selected Essays of James Britton

JANET EMIG
*The Web of Meaning: Essays on Writing, Teaching, Learning,
and Thinking*

JAMES MOFFETT
Coming on Center: English Education in Evolution

DONALD M. MURRAY
*Learning by Teaching: Selected Articles on Writing
and Teaching*

Contents

Introduction

Janet Emig

The Development of Writing Abilities, 11–18, The London group's major collaborative work, reveals their shared characteristics: width and subtlety of conceptualization; easy commerce with significant theory—Kelly, Langer, Luria, Polanyi, Vygotsky; jargon-free, even studiously unpretentious diction; richness and aptness of internationally drawn examples; and immense regard and respect for both teachers and children as colleagues and collaborators.

What in this inquiry of wide scope into languaging among children attracts Nancy Martin? This anthology of essays, thematically, even developmentally arranged, provides a rich response. Overarching is her interest in extending the characterization of the spectator role as defined by D. W. Harding and tellingly extended by James Britton. As the conclusion of "Children and Stories" she provides a comment on that role and, inevitably, because the two are intertwined, a definition of literature as well:

> ... one is continually a spectator (through listening or telling) of one's own and other people's lives, and ... this whole universe of story, in all its manifestations, is what literature is.

Such a view of literature—generous, encompassing—wars with the majority academic view in England and America that literature consists of texts written for the many by the few, a very stringently defined few. The position held by most departments of literature is one of unabashed and unswerving elitism, and of historical over-detail, a belief that it is more significant to discover the shop in Trieste where Joyce may have bought his underwear than to read, much less appreciate, the total written outpourings of all the children in Trieste, New York, and London. Theoretically, it is to set Harding and Britton and Rosenblatt against Leavis and Brooks and Warren.

Inside her conception of the spectator role, what is it that Nancy Martin takes seriously? As her section outline makes clear, talking for learning; ascertaining the purpose for stories, both those that children write and tell, as well as those told to them; writing for learning (across the curriculum); and delineating the interplay among intentions, models, and contexts.

To take each of these in turn: Historically, at least from Dartmouth on, the British have revealed an earlier and more thoughtful appreciation that learning for us all is grounded in talk, and talk of a special kind. The kind of talk under consideration is expressive talk, in everyday versus school or academic register. Developmentally, talk, of course, is irrepressible, except for that miniscule minority, who, for physiological or psychological reasons are mute. We know from Luria that talking for learning among young children is synpractic, a necessary concomitant of action—indeed a mode of action. To be silenced in schools, therefore, and to be divorced from their earliest idiom, the expressive, is for many children to lose their only access to academic learning.

Espousing an enlarged role for expressive talk in schools makes for a change, not only in the child's access to learning, but also in the roles available to the teacher—from grammar arbiter and linguistic gatekeeper to invitation giver and "instigator of awareness . . . of the need for different kinds of language in different situations," of becoming the one who provides, simply, training in genuine rhetoric. The approach also provides Americans and other colonists with new and needed training not merely in taking talk seriously, but in learning how to analyze tape and script to discern, in what initially seem diffused and unfocused ramblings, learning taking place. In Nancy Martin's useful metaphor, through analysis, the transcript "comes into focus like a slide under a microscope."

In "Children and Stories: Their Own and Other People's," she asks what such stories *do* for children. She answers this question, through an analysis grounded in Susanne Langer, of a story by a six year old Toronto boy whose father had deserted the family:

> Without the experience of stories told to him he would have had no familiar form on which to improvise his own symbolic transformation of his encounter with loss and grief. In transforming these events and emotions into a story he was making them more knowable and also distancing them.

She notes the double movement, only superficially paradoxical, toward involvement with primary material and aesthetic separation and necessary dispassion that Moffett noted so well in *Teaching the Universe of Discourse* (1968), and that recently (1982) Thomas Newkirk so brilliantly documents in "Anatomy of a Breakthrough," his case study of Ann, New Hampshire college freshman, and abused child.

There follow two sections in which she sets forth extensions and implications of the two Schools Council Writing projects; a child-script-substantiated discussion of audience and function categories; and a portfolio for three ages of children—6–7, 9–10, and 10–11—that reveals these in action. Again, what is interesting to this one American spectator is the early ethnographic emphasis, the collection and analysis of what is, rather than of what could or should be.

Next, she entertains perhaps the most pervasive question even of those willing to begin with the expressive, "Yes, I'm willing to begin where they begin; but everyone knows where any school writer must end and that is by demonstrating her competence as a good transactional writer. Describe the journey from *a* to *b*, or *z*." And so she does, with two writing case studies from the upper school, to demonstrate

> that the way into it is not by recipe but by the constant interaction of a personal viewpoint with information from varied secondary sources. We think this dynamic is the actual process of learning as well as of language growth.

Perhaps her most significant contribution through these essays is that represented in her most recent work: "Next Directions," with its consideration of the role of intention in the process of writing, and, again, almost simultaneously because these matters are intertwined, the roles of models and contexts; for, as she points out, "language exists in a context of immediate use . . . and is therefore rooted in a context of meaning."

Drawing on the Writing Across the Curriculum project, as well as on the work of Jerome Bruner, Lucy Calkins, Donald Graves, Richard Lloyd-Jones and others, she gives the necessary attribute of any generative curriculum—a setting, a context where children of all ages come to master the transactional mode. In such a setting, learning and writing begin with primary experience recorded in journals; with individual choices of topics; with models available, defined not as "something to be consciously imitated" but as "an item whose use and form are recognized by repeated encounters"; and with teachers who respond as advisers and trusted critics. Eloquently she notes:

> "If intention is the motivating force for thinking as well as action, then creativity in a very general sense would seem to be related to intention. If we could accept some kind of balance between the teachers' intentions (programs, syllabuses, etc.) and those of the students, we should have something like co-operative learning/teaching."

I

Talking and Learning

Learning to talk is a recognized triumph for the learner, though talking itself is not always seen for what it is—the starting point and continuing agent of learning. Ironically, however, children's everyday language—the chief continuing agent of their learning—can come into conflict with the language of education. What happens then?

1

So All Talk Is Significant

Conversation is universally interesting. " 'What is the use of a book,' thought Alice, 'without pictures or conversations?' " Indeed, as we go about our daily lives, we all engage in a kind of universal spectatorship as we tell and listen to the hundreds of small tales and anecdotes which form the fabric of the largest part of our conversations. Operations, lost luggage, missed trains, bus stop encounters; quarrels, injustices, griefs, romances; what he said and what she said. We literally tell the stories of our lives—their prospect and their retrospect—as we live them. And, of course, we comment on these happenings, discuss the rights and wrongs and speculate on general matters in the process of constructing the realities of our lives in conversation.

Most of us are chiefly familiar with children's conversation as it comes to us as adults. We have little opportunity of listening to their talk to each other, so it may come as a surprise to find how long and how far children who have been sent off on their own to explore a poem or rehearse a talk for a class audience will go. They will sometimes talk together for 40 minutes about one poem, or a single incident from a story, or until the tape runs out. Teachers themselves would probably be wary of spending so long on a single task for fear of losing the attention of their pupils, but the children on their own appear to have no such qualms. Perhaps this is only surprising because adults largely control the lives of children, and in schools and families probably initiate more talk than the children do when the two generations are in social contact. Thus the patterns of daily living are on the whole determined by us, as adults, as are the patterns of talk that go with

An adapted version of the Introduction to *Understanding Children Talking*. Penguin Books Ltd., 1976.

them; but outside these patterns of behavior and talk is the children's "underground movement" when they are not in contact with adults and where their talk does not closely follow adult norms. They are now the initiators, and they are not short of language or ideas. We have known for some time that children can write extremely well, but we know relatively little about their capacities for talking.

Most of us are accustomed to reading what has been *written to be read;* when we read a transcript of *speech* it strikes us as unfamiliar and we are not sure where to put our attention. We may enter the "conversation" in imagination as if we were actually present—all our attention focused on the meanings being exchanged by the speakers, which, of course, is what we mostly do when we engage in talk ourselves. But we may—as sometimes momentarily in actual conversations—shift our focus of attention to concentrate on the task itself and become observers rather than listeners. If we do this we perceive some startling things. The actual grammatical structure, for instance, of spoken language in the children's conversations is likely to give us our first shock; and the next one may be to find that adult conversations are very similar in this respect. Then there is the fact that many things other than the words uttered are always part of these conversations. Speakers pick up points, make statements or ask questions which, although they are within the terms of the conversation, reflect individual interests or preoccupations. In short, transcripts of speech, although presented in written form, are not written language at all, and what they reveal at first is the startling fact that the spoken language is extremely different from the written language. This fact tends to come as a shock to people unused to reading transcripts of speech.

Moreover, there are assumptions behind the comments derived from contemporary studies of the spoken language, and these sometimes run counter to popular ideas about speech. For instance, people tend to distinguish "useful" talk from "mere" talk. People often say *"that* discussion got nowhere," or "what was that speech all about? I didn't get much from it," but it does not usually occur to them to make such judgments about most of the talk that goes on most of the time, because their expectations are different. In the case of "useful" talk, there is some kind of transaction afoot; people want information, or want to convince someone else, to argue, explain or inform, and, according to whether their expectations are fulfilled or not, they judge the talk useful or "pointless." But it may not be so judged by other participants. Everyone has the choice of speaking or remaining silent, and in this sense all utterances must be purposive for the speaker, though the listener may not find them so. So the distinction would seem to lie more in the circumstances in which the talk arises than in some hard and fast difference between purposive and purposeless talk. The interaction between the members of a group talking together determines whether the conversation is switched on to an "engage for action" position or to "relax"; and people learn which situation they are in without its ever being made explicit. Of course, we sometimes make mistakes. If, for instance, in a conversation where people are grumbling or letting off steam, one proposes to take action, one can be met by a sudden silence. The unspoken social terms of the conversation have been misinterpreted. The switch has been in the "relax" position, and the other participants did not really want it switched over to "engage." Similarly, when one's expectations are for some speech transaction to be fulfilled, and other people have no such expectations, one comes away saying that the talk was pointless, or that no one was serious.

Another feature of speech situations which profoundly affects the kind of talk that goes on is the size of the group. Conversation is talk between two or a few people. If the group gets much larger and attempts to talk together, either some people remain silent, or two or three begin to have a separate conversation. Furthermore, conversation proceeds from the interaction of the various speakers, so its course is socially determined and is therefore very different from the course of a public speech or a class lesson.

Let's look at the difference between talk in large and small groups more closely. The course of conversation, or small-group talk, is unpredictable. No one knows at the beginning where it will go or at what point it will end. A person may have something particular to ask or to tell, but beyond this no one knows until it happens. The course of the conversation is mutually determined *as it goes.* What happens in large groups is entirely different. A single person gives a speech, or a lecture or a sermon, but all these are in fact monologues which represent a single speaker's extended and coherent utterance directed to some particular end. It is often predictable what this utterance will be about in general, and it is also generally accepted that the listeners will not contribute to the talk until the speaker has finished—or they may not contribute at all.

In school there is, of course, much conversation, but most schools are organized in large group units, i.e. classes, and teachers do a good deal of class teaching (or talking). In certain kinds of class lesson, the talk is fan-shaped, with the teacher at the hub of the fan sending out questions and receiving replies from the other speakers who are scattered along the vanes of the fan, as it were. The talk is like this, of course, because its purpose is to instruct a large group, and it is not essentially different in function from a speech, a lecture, or a sermon. The teacher, like the public speaker, generally has his construct of what the talk is going to be about and by his questions he draws from the children only the responses which will develop his construct, and it is the dynamic of the teacher's initial frame of reference which determines the course of the lesson. Sometimes this sort of lesson gets off course when children initiate their own questions or ideas, but eventually the teacher will say "Well, now, let's get back to the point"—his point in this case, not necessarily the point for all his listeners.

Thus, in work situations, talk is seen as performing some mutual transaction, whether in large groups or small groups and by means of lectures, class teaching or conversation. And it is this situation of an expected talk transaction that people refer to when they say the talk was useful, or pointless, or not serious, etc.

But a great deal of the talk that goes on in our daily lives is not of this kind, and at first sight seems not to have any particular purpose. Consider, for instance, the phenomenon of the way we sometimes go over a television program or a film we have liked, and others who have seen it join in a kind of collective re-creation of it. Clearly we are not doing this to inform each other, since all parties have seen it. And we have noted earlier the way we exchange the tales of our daily lives. Nothing is too trivial to be recounted if the teller sees it as significant. What is it all in aid of? What is the function of all those apparently purposeless conversations when the social switch is on "relax"? There are a number of theories and partial theories which can be used to interpret the content and function of such talk; but as yet, no theory of sufficient generality has emerged which will fully explain this most ordinary of activities.

Rushing in, I would suggest that we all need to work through, sort, organize and evaluate the events of our daily lives. Sleeping, we do this in dreams; waking, in internal monologues and relaxed talk. As individuals we have to assimilate our experiences and build them into our continuing picture of the world; as social beings we need to legitimize the world picture we are continuously constructing and maintaining. So we hold out to others—in talk—our observations, discoveries, reflections, opinions, attitudes and values; and the responses we receive in the course of these conversations profoundly affect both the world picture we are creating and our view of ourselves.

Seen thus, all talk is significant and is the chief means by which we develop as individual and social beings. Furthermore, from this perspective, the difference between what we began by calling purposive talk and apparently random talk is only of importance in that it enables us, in general, to look at the whole conversation of mankind in all its variety and to see it all as an educative process. And perhaps we should add that an overemphasis on purposive talk must necessarily militate against relaxed talk and the opportunities this offers for the growth of self-knowledge.

There is a further question: Children spend much of their lives in school and school has been traditionally concerned with formal education. Should teachers be concerned with a process like conversation which goes on universally anyway? Viewed developmentally, we can say that talk grows as we grow. The question is, can we use talk to assist the growing?

To answer this question we need to consider the relation of talk to thinking, to learning (in its school sense) and other school activities such as writing, doing experiments, and engaging in practical work of all sorts.

In the earliest stages of language learning, talk and objects and actions are indivisible. Toddlers name things and ask for things and give orders and make utterances about things they have seen or about people; and one word may have to do all these things, for example "dog." When they begin to refer to things that happened yesterday or that are not present and part of their immediate surroundings, they have made a huge step forward in language learning and in intellectual growth: they have learned to dissociate their speech from the here and now, and have begun to be aware of the past and the future. Parents will be familiar with the imagined situations children create by means of language around their playthings. Later they can create imagined situations without the help of playthings and can engage in stories, monologues, dramas and "poems" where they construct an oral, verbal "object" arising from their experience and feelings which is organized and sustained by language alone. It is from this kind of spoken utterance that imaginative writing develops. The significance of these utterances is that they are the chief mode by which young children think. For instance, most of the "Once upon a time" stories which they invent are disguised versions of their own experiences. Parallel to this process is the development of social communicative speech—speech for others, as distinct from speech for oneself, though these two processes may sometimes be seen going on side by side.

It could be argued that by the time children are seven or eight they have learned to use the basic systems of speech and are also, broadly speaking, literate, and therefore talk could be left to look after itself and teachers concentrate on the more difficult matter of developing children's capacities to use the written language (reading and writing) together with the knowledge that resides in it. A more sociological view would provide a different answer. A bird's eye look at the situations in which different kinds of talk happen shows that these do not occur universally. A school could be, and we think should be, an environment in which all kinds of talk do in fact happen; where children can talk to adults in both formal and informal situations, where purposive, or directed talk goes on—as it always has—and where undirected and unconstrained conversations are also seen as part of the educative process. And here we want to take the argument a stage further, and suggest that ordinary talk has an important part to play in the assimilation of new knowledge and new experience.

New knowledge has to be fitted in to existing knowledge, to be translated into terms of one's own experience and reinterpreted, and in this process (which can be called learning) thought and language are very close together. But thought is of great density and speed, and much of it is not within conscious control. If any of it is to be made coherent and communicative, a ready-at-hand language is needed to net and give initial shape to the transient flow of ideas, perceptions, images, feelings. One's everyday speech is the nearest-at-hand language that everyone has and is therefore particularly appropriate for new learning situations and first formulations, first drafts of new thinking. And since what has to be sorted out and reinterpreted is not the same for everyone, wide-ranging conversations may well be just what a group of speakers needs. What is regarded as a rambling irrelevancy to one person may be a central sorting-out operation to another. But one can only do this sorting out in one's own language, which is the nearest one can come—in the initial stages—to one's own thinking. Furthermore, any attempt at this stage to divert a speaker from *what* he is saying to *how* he is saying it will be a diversion in his thinking. The very features which characterize everyday speech—its looseness, its relative inexplicitness, its focus on the speaker's own vision—themselves give access to thinking. Thus, it would seem that everyday speech should be seen as the matrix from which one moves into other modes when they are needed, and to which one reverts in new or difficult situations. This would mean that teachers could not only rest easy with their pupils' everyday language for much more of the time than most of them now think is appropriate, but they could encourage it and create situations where it could occur, knowing its importance to a learner.

This, however, is not the whole story. The "models" of language (spoken and written) that we encounter all the time, without, of course, seeing them as models, are a major influence on our language development. Children's speech approximates to the dominant influences in their lives—their homes, their local community, street, village or school; later it will approximate to other adult models coming from work, peer groups, or deliberate approximation to particular speakers. But within schools, or perhaps within education more generally—in text books, and notes, in the specialized terms and conventions of different subjects and in most teachers' modes of presentation—are the models in which public knowledge is *presented* to children: a very different language, as we have suggested above, from the language in which one explores knowledge for oneself in talk. Most children find it a difficult language to read and more difficult still to write. Their stumbling, inert sentences can be seen in any school notebook, but what is often forgotten is that children are not professional historians and scientists but learners, and we would suggest that they are often pushed too hard and too soon towards these imitations of adult transactional language without regard for the needs of the actual situation, which is of their learning.

In conclusion, there are good reasons why every kind of talk should go on in schools, but what is crucial in learning is a respect for each child's vernacular, whatever it may be—a respect for everyday speech.

2

In Their Own Words:

The Potential of Everyday Language

Parents are notorious for repeating laughable or extraordinary things their children have said, but the utterances often are laughable and do seem extraordinary, so it is not only parental pride which makes children's speech a topic of conversation among adults. Many teachers too get a lot of pleasure out of things that children say but they are also troubled by an uneasy sense that this sort of thing won't do for school, or won't do for life: that it's too enjoyable or playful or unorthodox for the earnest business of education. We want to ask: Why won't it do? Is something more than a Puritan ethic involved? If so, is it possible to identify what everyday language can do and can't do? May there be, for instance, reasons connected with the nature of everyday language which make it ineffective for some purposes, or is the uneasiness that teachers feel about it derived from social attitudes about dialects vis-a-vis standard English—or teacherly attitudes towards the virtue of what is difficult?

This debate has, of course, been rumbling away for a long time with periodic eruptions in letters and articles in the educational press, and it was sharply focused by the publication of *Language, the Learner and the School.** The issue raised was the gap between what might loosely be called "the language of education" and children's everyday language. It has been generally taken for granted that this gap should be closed by having children acquire as soon as possible the "language of education."

To answer in part the question of what everyday language can and can't do, we need to look more closely at what is meant by "everyday lan-

Published in the *Times Educational Supplement,* May 17, 1974.
*Douglas Barnes, James Britton, and Harold Rosen. *Language, the Learner and the School.* Penguin, 1969 for the London Association for the Teaching of English. Revised editions, 1970 and 1983.

guage" and the "language of education." But first a more general point about language.

Models and Innovations

Behind the debate about everyday language versus other kinds lies the central paradox of language itself. Language faces two ways, outwards and inwards. Its outward face spans the generations and holds relatively constant the common forms and common meanings developed, on the one hand, by speakers of English everywhere, and on the other hand, by different speech communities within the English speaking world—regions, cities, work groups, for instance. Its inward face is towards everyone's individual experience, which never exactly coincides with anyone else's. So each of us has to use the public or common forms of language (sounds, words and sentence patterns) to express the unique meanings of individual experience. A tiger is a tiger to everyone, but everyone's tiger is slightly different. When you come to words like *home,* or *democracy* or *culture,* the area of differing meanings is much greater. Words don't have stable meanings though some are more stable than others.

Daring Innovators

The opposition between common forms and new utterances is the dynamic by which we learn our mother tongue. The successful resolution of these oppositions is an individual "voice," which can confidently share its meanings with others, and is able to move towards a more public voice, or a more individual voice, according to the needs of different purposes and people. Both directions are necessarily part of one's education, in school and out, but in school they tend to be seen as polarizations instead of contraries which nourish each other. For different reasons children and poets are the most daring innovators in language; for instance:

> the birds nest is warm
> the feather on its chest is soft and fluffy and spongy and red when the
> feather drops on the hand it is nothing.
>
> Sally, 6 years.

Children are naturally curious, playful, and ambitious in their experiments with language; they make their own versions of things they want to say more boldly than adults do, but at the same time, like adults, they draw continuously on the models they meet—at home, in school, and in their streets and villages.

If, within the general picture of the way an individual advances into his mother tongue, we now look at everyday speech, we can say about it, in general, that it is local, comfortable, and above all, ready-at-hand: you can relax in it or work with it, and if you maltreat it or beautify it a bit, no one bothers because everyone is familiar with variations in everyday speech from encounters with people from different towns or regions. If we also look at the language of education (classroom speech and school writing), we find that it draws particularly on "standard" English, which is a prestigious class dialect, and on the public forms of the written language. A lot of time in school is concerned with the written language; children read a lot and write a lot, and some of this rubs off on the speech used in classrooms, while the generalized and impersonal forms of public writing provide the model which most teachers set up for their students.

It is on the personal and expressive aspects of everyday language, spoken or written, that we will now focus. Expressive language reflects the way we respond to people or situations; it reflects *ourselves*, our thoughts, feelings, and attitudes. It has a negative pole, when we feel the need to defend ourselves and attack others. In this situation the speech is directed *at* rather than *to* someone else, and expresses emotions and thoughts (anger, grief, aggression, for instance) which only take account of the listener as someone to be spoken at and not as a human being with human needs. This kind of expressive language reflects the self in its least social aspects. At the other pole the speaker approaches someone else with his defenses down: he takes for granted an interest and trust from his listener so that he is not at risk in uttering his thoughts and feelings. He may express outrageous opinions or tentative half-formed thoughts and uncertain attitudes, and he can only do this when he does not risk a rebuff.

Furthermore, this kind of expressive language assumes that much of the background of the utterance is shared with the listener, so the speaker does not need to be particularly explicit. This leaves the speaker freer to express more of the mercurial quality of thought, and this in turn is reflected in a relative looseness of structure.

First Drafts of New Thinking

The first point to note is concerned with the density of thought and the speed with which thoughts happen, and with the fact that most of these mental events are not within conscious control. If any of this is to be made coherent and communicable, a ready-at-hand language is needed to net and give initial shape to the transient flow of thoughts, perceptions, images, feelings. Everyday speech is the nearest-at-hand language that anyone has and is therefore particularly suitable for exploratory learning and for first drafts of new thinking. Consider, for instance, the following utterance:

Trevor composes (with a tape recorder) a talk on the development of man.

. . . . Now you see this sort of apish thing began to develop in more than one way. It was developing to walk on its hind legs very stooped,

so that it went down on its four legs occasionally. . . . but it also. . . .
what else was developing which was apart from the dinosaurs that was
developed and some of the other mammals. . . . it developed in its
brain. Its brain developed very . . . it sort of developed with its body,
you know, it went with its body. . . .

Trevor, 12 years.

The very features which characterize expressive language—its looseness, its
relative inexplicitness, its focus on the speaker's own vision—themselves
give access to thinking; any attempt at this stage to divert a speaker from
what he is saying to *how* he is saying it will be a diversion to his thinking.

Thus it would seem that expressive language should be seen as the
base from which we move into other modes when they are needed, and to
which we revert in new or difficult situations. This would mean that teachers of all subjects could rest easy with their pupils' everyday language for
much more of the time than most of them now think is appropriate, and
they could also encourage it, and create situations where it could occur,
knowing its importance to a learner.

School Writing: Freedom to Think

However, this is not the whole story. Many teachers do accept the importance of everyday speech, but when it comes to writing, the picture
changes. Writing in school is a big industry, and children, like most adults,
approach it with a sigh. It does present special problems. The most teasing
of these is the question we began with: Are there things that written everyday language can't do well enough? Certainly, children are discouraged
from drawing on the rich resources of everyday language in their school
writing. For instance, they (and adults too) often pursue an argument or
explore an abstract idea in terms of personal reminiscence, or dramatic accounts of actual dialogue, or they address the reader directly, or include
asides to themselves, as Nigel does in the following excerpt from his essay:

. . . . I find being able to put my views down on paper and being entirely unrestricted in what i say helps a fantastic amount with what i
write which so aids the other reasons i gave for writing. In the first
year of my secondary schooling i did not have this freedom to express
myself, this i found very frustrating because i always thought that
what we were being told to do was completely worth-less—which it
may or may not have been but i am sure i get a lot more out of what i
write now than what i did then.

Nigel, 14 years.

In the school context students are required to write impersonal, often
generalized and abstract language. What we don't know is the extent to
which this kind of language is a power or a hindrance to their thinking.

One of the values of abstractions would seem to be that they enable us to hold disparate notions together and thereby to think at a more general level. Everyday language probably won't allow this kind of condensation of thought.

Two questions, however, arise from this: first, can children move into this kind of thinking and language as quickly and directly as the prevalent mode in school writing assumes? And second, to what extent is this mode only a convention, a kind of exercise to prepare them for reading this kind of language? We are, of course, talking about only one kind of writing; that is, writing concerned with classification, comparison, and explanation. But as a number of surveys have shown, this kind of writing dominates the schools. Probably the most that we can say at present is that all students should be encouraged to draw on all their resources—from their everyday speech, from reading, from listening and watching—and the test of what they write should be the extent to which it is a genuine communication. As things are now, some children, the majority, in fact, suffer more than others from the domination of expositional writing.

However, the potential of everyday language for learning is not the only point in the debate. People say, "If you can't speak standard English you are at a disadvantage in the job market. Everyone ought to have the chance to speak 'properly'," or, "If teachers don't teach proper English, who will?" These expressions of anxiety reflect widespread and powerfully-felt opinions in all sections of society. What is really being debated is whether some people's everyday speech is an inferior form of language. Linguists say that every speech community develops a language which is adequate to its needs, and that one language cannot be said to be superior to another, but when people from different speech communities meet, the one which is deemed superior will also be thought to have superior speech. This is clearly a matter of social attitudes and has little to do with the intrinsic quality of language, but it has powerful side effects. Confidence is all-important in learning, and if you have come to believe that every time you open your mouth you declare yourself inferior, you soon take to silence.

The social argument is a powerful one because it has economic roots growing from our English pattern of culture and it seems to lead to an impasse. It might be resolved if we could look at language more broadly and accept children's everyday speech as their main base of operations; and it needs to be seen as an adult as well as a childish function of language. But there are many other functions of language and other audiences than those to whom expressive language is addressed. Children need to meet as wide a range of these situations as possible which would give them opportunities to use language in all sorts of ways, taking what they want from their reading and experimenting in their usage as freely as most children do before they go to school.

Given some such overall view of the dimensions and possibilities of language use, a teacher would have a different and bigger role to play than just being someone who teaches a subject and the "proper" language of that subject. Whatever his subject, he would be a setter-up of situations in which different kinds of language would be expected and encouraged; he would be a deliberate provider of different language models; and he would be the instigator of an awareness in his pupils of the need for different kinds of language in different situations. In effect, he would be developing language policies for his different classes.

Such a view of language function in relation to children's development would see expressive language as the core of a child's "universe of discourse" and would allow it to feed into learning at all levels. A new respect for everyday language is needed.

II

Transformations
of Experience:
Stories and Poems

Stories are a kind of fable, transformations of experience which you could unpick if you knew enough about the storyteller; but what would be the point? The transformation, the fable, the story is the point. And it is the story which transforms the listeners into active spectators busily integrating the story they have just heard into their own life pictures. Who is the teller and who the listener? Spectators all.

3

Children and Stories:

Their Own and Other People's

Everyone knows that stories are like spells. Someone fixes you with a glittering eye and you have to listen, but in fact the Ancient Mariner told his story chiefly for himself—to lay the ghost that was haunting him. "Chiefly for himself": what do their own stories do for children? What are they really about? Who are the characters—the clown, or the wolf or the lost boy? And what do the stories the children listen to or read do for them?

This article on children and stories is a follow-up from a detailed study which was made of the kinds of written language that children use and encounter in primary school (Martin 1972). That analysis of a week's output from three different classes in three different schools threw up some interesting facts. When the children wrote stories, for instance, these were longer than anything else they wrote and the language was more complex. Again, while they were obviously much influenced by the form of the stories they had read or listened to, in content—however disguised—they seemed to be about themselves, their lives, and the people who were important to them. So, in this article we attempt to say something about the function and educational importance of stories by exploring the contexts in which the stories printed here were told, written, listened to or read.

The first one comes from a Toronto elementary school where the children (aged six to seven) told stories to their teacher and she typed them up in big type on long wall-strips and the children illustrated them as they wished. A six-year-old boy from Jesse Catcham school wrote:

Published in *Classroom Encounters: Language and English Teaching*, M. Torbe and R. Protherough (eds.), Ward Lock Educational, 1976.

My story

Once upon a time there was a little boy, and he didn't have a mother or father. One day he was walking in the forest. He saw a rabbit. It led him to a house. There was a book inside of the house. He looked at the book and saw a pretty animal. It was called a "horse".

He turned the page and saw a picture of a rabbit . . . a rabbit just like he had seen in the forest. He turned the page again and saw a cat. He thought of his mother and father, and when he was small and they had books for him, and animals for him to play with. He thought about this . . . and he started to cry. While he was crying a lady said, "What's the matter, boy?"
He slowly looked around and saw his mother.
He said, "Is it really you?"
"Yes, my son. I'm your mother."
"Mother, mother . . . are you alive?"
"No child. This is the house that I was killed in."
"Oh mother . . . why are you here?"
"Because I came back to look for you."
"Why mother? Why did you come to look for me?"
"Because I miss you."
"Where is father?"
"He is in the coffin that he was buried in. But don't talk about that now. How are you son? You're bigger . . . and I'm glad to see you."
"It's been a long time mother."
While the boy and the mother were talking his father came into the room and said,
"Hi, son. How are you?"
"Fine," said the boy, "fine."
Suddenly the mother and father came to life.
The boy was crying, and the mother and father were crying too. God suddenly gave them a miracle . . . to come to life. The boy looked at the mother and father and said, "Oh mother, oh father."

We know something of the background of this story. The boy lived alone with his mother because the father had deserted them some six months before this story was written. It begins, as the stories he has listened to often began, "Once upon a time there was a little boy, and he didn't have a mother or a father. . . . " The conventional start with its attendant circumstances—the forest, the rabbit, the house in the woods. These lead him straight into his feelings of loss and desolation and he wrote, not a story about a deserted family, but a dream-like conversation with a lady who declares herself his dead mother come back to look for him. As they talk, his dead father comes into the room and greets him. "God suddenly gave them a miracle. . . . The boy looked at the mother and father and said, 'Oh mother, oh father.' " Even at six, miracles belong to reality in a way that dreams do not, and the miracle allowed him to bring his parents back to life in an ending which provided not only the way he wanted things to be, but also the way he felt a story needed to end. Without the experience of stories told to him he would have had no familiar form on which to improvise his own symbolic transformation of his encounter with loss and grief. In transforming these events and emotions into a story, he was making them more knowable, and also distancing them. Few of us can speak directly of grief. It is not only children of six who need to speak through stories or poems, or to allow stories or poems to speak their grief for them. The stories that children make (if they are left undirected) are not whimsical inventions but a kind of fable about things that concern them, but re-shaped, so that events are more as the author would have them be. Against the background of this view of the origination of children's stories let's look at *Bedtime*, written by a girl of twelve who had been in institutions or with various foster parents since she was a baby, and had never known a family life of her own.

> I am in bed
>   in bed—
>   Almost asleep—
>   But not quite.
>   There's Peggy
>   Cleaning her teeth
>   Over by the bathroom.
>   George slams his door—
>   He's in bed now.
>   Monica calls to mother
>   "What shall I wear?"
>   She is going out,
>   Lucky thing!
>
> Monica's big,
> I am small;
> She goes out
> I do not.
> The front door slams—
> Monica's gone.
> George, Peggy,
> And I are in bed.

The stairs creak
Mother comes
Says "Goodnight"
And goes to bed.
A solitary cat
Mews on the tiles,
One lone dog howls
Miserably.
A hooting owl flies
Silently overhead.

All is still
All is safe
All is quiet.

Henrietta Dombey makes a comment on these "stories" in another kind of language when she writes about a lonely and neglected boy in one of her classes called Gwyn, who came to school one day and said to her, "Me cat died, Miss: can you find me a story about a cat, Miss? When you read something it helps you sort it out in your mind."

We suggest that the makers of the first two stories printed here were helping themselves "in their minds" by the stories they had made, in the same way that Gwyn was trying to help himself by seeking comfort from reading a story about a cat. But he knew the power of stories. Not all children have the early encounters with stories which teach them this. When they do have these encounters they find they have a form which they can use to represent and share their transformations and rearrangements of experience.

These "stories" arose from the dark side of life. The other wall picture-stories from Jesse Catcham school were funny and joyous, but also seemed to be about how the children would *like* things to be. It is impossible to reproduce Midget Mugsey (spoken by Michel and typed by his teacher) which was fifteen feet in length and extended down the wall and across the floor with integrated text and pictures. A circus midget would be about the size of a six-year-old, so one can see why he was so popular as a hero, but a real midget is part of the grown up world—as Midget Mugsey was in the story—and could do tricks, get money, have adventures, control fierce dogs and ride a galloping black horse.

Adults write stories like this for children, and children also make them up for themselves, but the business of learning what a story is, and what an "article" is, or what a report is, or a salesman's talk, or a prayer, is chiefly learnt unconsciously by encountering them in their different contexts. Stories are met very early in life because in the form of anecdotes they happen at all times and all places. Furthermore, narrative comes in chronological sequence and this is the sequence of our lives. For that reason stories are easy to perceive and the "fabulous" nature of the characters makes them powerful and therefore memorable.

The following conversations from a Durham nursery school show something of the early processes when children begin to penetrate what it means to be a spectator of other people's lives. Here is a three-year-old exploring what a story is:

The handbag story

Helen held her teacher's hand and whispered:

H: Miss Evans, tell Mrs. Tindale to tell us the handbag story.

T: I don't think I know that story.

H: You do.

T: Do you mean to ask Mrs. Tindale to show you what is inside her handbag?

H: Yes.

T: That's not a story. It's talking about the things in her handbag.

H: It is a story. It's the story of all the things. And every time it's a different story.

T: I never thought of it as a story. Is it a story when we talk about the birds in the garden, when we feed them and make bird cakes for them?

H: No, silly.

T: Why is that not the story of the birds?

H: Because . . . because . . . we *did* it. *You* have to *tell* us about things. The birds come and they eated all the things up and we watched. Mrs. Tindale *tells* about her things. Are you going to tell her to tell us . . . now?

T: We'll both go and ask Mrs. Tindale if she will find some time today to tell you her handbag story.

Few adults would think of the narrative sequence of pulling items out of a handbag one by one and talking about them as constituting a story, but narrative sequence is not all that is involved. Helen seems to make a more fundamental distinction when she distinguishes between "doing" and "telling." Miss Evans asks her why their activities and talk about the birds as they fed them was not a story and Helen replies ". . . because we *did* it. *You* have to *tell* us about things. The birds come and they eated all the things. Mrs. Tindale *tells* us about her things. . . ." (author's italics). So a story is telling; there has to be a narrator as well as a narrative sequence, but Helen's sense of what is a story (on this occasion at least) is founded in what is there in her physical presence—objects and a narrative within touching distance.

The next dialogue from this nursery shows a sudden enlargement of the children's notions about stories. Alex and Rachel each had a teething ring, one of which had attached to it a white lamb, the other a yellow duck. After some talk about the lamb and the duck Miss Evans told them the story of the ugly duckling.

R: But he wasn't a duck. He was a swan. Is this a duck?

T: Yes, yours is a young duck and he's called a duckling.

R: I want a story about a duckling.

A: I want a story about my lamb.

T: Didn't you tell me they both lived on the same farm?

R: Mm

A: (nods)

Then followed an impromptu story about a lamb and a duckling.

R: Did you know that story?

T: No.

A: You did. You said it.

R: Did you just make it up?

T: That's right.

R: How did you know what to say? It must have been true.

T: No, I looked at the lamb and the duck, thought about them living on the same farm in summer time. Then I imagined the sort of thing I would do if I had been a lamb or a duck.

R: (dragging Alex away) Come on, I'm going to be a duck.

Next day.

J: Rachel says you can make up a story about anything.

T: Well, not anything. Some things might be a bit difficult.

J: Rachel says you told her a story about her duck and Alex's lamb. I want a true story about my Patch. I'll just go and get the others so wait before you start.

R: We're going to have a story called "Patch", aren't we Miss Evans? Don't you make them up? My daddy says only teachers can make them up. I asked him last night, but he can't. And my mummy cannot either.

There followed a story about Patch, and another about the push chair, and another . . . and another . . .

Much later

R: Did you read my story somewhere about my Dilly?

T: No, I just thought it in my head.

R: Was it not true anyway? Will you read it sometime?

T: It isn't written anywhere for me to read.

R: Will you write it?

T: Yes, I'll have it tomorrow.

Next day, the typed story was presented to Rachel.

R: Is this it?
T: This is the story. Should I read it to you?
R: It's not the story. It cannot be the story on there.
T: Why not?
R: It's not a book. So it's not a proper story.

So these children were learning that not all stories are the stories of actual lives, that people can imagine events and characters and weave these into a story, that this story can not only be told but can also be written down and read aloud.

And, of course, the stories that children read, or that teachers read to them, perform similar functions to those that they write themselves. Elizabeth Grugeon tells of a book called *The Orphans of Simitra* which she read to her class. This was about some Greek children in war time sent for safety to Holland which they hated for its rain and cold and difference from their own country. She found the following two pieces of unsolicited writing in the rough book of an eleven-year-old Cypriot girl.

The two children
the dear children there hartes must be full of tears, moveing from there own Simitre and then to holland now alfal and throw in the loss of thier parents and brother and haveing to look after each other and now more trouble has come up mina has run away and pophius is looking for her. "She was not to be found" poor mina will she ever be found all there is left to do was search and cherch—"but was she to be found"

Simitra
Two poems in one

the skys are so blue
the flowers so gay
the mountains
and hills so high and bright
Just like the month of
May

Holland

the skys are so Grey
the flowers so dull
the hills and mountains
are not to be seen
and the road are straight
as can be

It is difficult to track down the effect of the stories children read, but Gwyn's request to Mrs. Dombey to find him a story about a cat and these Cypriot writings are striking clues about some of the functions of literature. Grief can be distanced and to some extent exorcised by telling or writing or reading about it, but life is also for celebrating and mankind has to shake off the nightmare which myth has placed upon its chest (Benjamin 1973):

> The wisest thing—so the fairy tale taught mankind in olden times, and teaches children to this day—is to meet the forces of the mythical world with cunning and with high spirits ... the liberating magic which the fairy tale has at its disposal does not bring nature into play in a mythical way, but points to the tale's complicity with liberated man. A mature man feels this complicity only occasionally, that is, when he is happy; but the child first meets it in fairy tales, and it makes him happy.

The story of the boy who had to learn fear in Ruth Manning Saunders's *Book of Goblins and Witches* is a case in point and Heather Lyons quotes it—and others from this series—as being immensely popular in her classes. It is about a bold and practical boy who was not at all alarmed by a ghost which came down the chimney a limb at a time and interrupted him in his sausage-cooking. The story has its spine-chilling elements but it is above all a jokey story, and the cheek of the boy is what the listening children envy. Cunning and high spirits are the way to deal with ghosts.

Fairy stories and folk tales, of course, originated in a local context and were passed from mouth to mouth, and even when written down they keep the flavor and the characteristics of spoken stories. They are not consumable and everyone expects to hear them many times. Moreover anyone can (and people frequently do) add new bits to them or improvise their own versions to make them fit a new context. We can see this process at work in the account given by Mrs. Lyons of a girl in one of her classes who often used to entertain the class and the teacher by improvising stories about the class itself, and its teacher, and headmaster. Here is a transcript of one of these occasions—although the atmosphere of daring and conspiracy and humor is inevitably lost in the printed version. The story is part of a continuing serial about the terrible children of class 3HL and the troubles they caused their teacher (Mrs. Lyons) who called in the headmaster to intervene on more than one occasion. The names are real ones and class 3HL was Karen's class, but there the reality ends and fantasy begins.

Karen's story

'Goodbye.' She slammed the door. 'What was all that about?' she said. 'What have you been doing? Playing a trick on me, making me feel a fool?'

'Oh,' said Eileen, 'We sort of er—nothing ...'

'Don't,' said Mrs. Lyons. 'The next time this happens I *will* get Mr. Jenkins and he *will* sort you out.'

So—the next day, the children came in and Alan Massey started singing a song. He brought his electric guitar in and started singing *Harry Krishna* and all the top twenty. It was a racket—Bobby Gentry, Lew Christy, everybody you could think of. She—loves you—yeah—yeah—yeah! except it wasn't like that—it was sort of more like a foghorn. Mrs. Lyons thought 'This is my chance to get the headmaster.' So she ran into the headmaster's office 'Mr. Jenkins! Mr. Jenkins! Come quickly! My children are at it again!'

'Oh, are they?' said Mr. Jenkins.

'Yes,' she said. 'Quick, before they stop.'

But unfortunately Beverley Hall looks after the class in the window. 'Quick,' she said, 'they're coming. They're coming. 'Quick! Sit down!' she shouted.

Everyone sat down quickly doing their alpha beta.

'Mrs. Lyons!' said the headmaster, 'Your children—have been as good as gold. Now what do you think of *this?*'

'B-b-but-' says Mrs. Lyons, 'th-they w-w-were . . .'

'Oh, *shut* up, woman!' said the headmaster. 'I'm going and don't waste any more of my time will you—Mrs. Lyons?'

'N-n-no' said Mrs. Lyons, amazed at the children. 'We-e-l-l. What was all that about?'

'Oh, well,' said Beverley, 'We sort of—um—' and all the boys and girls stood up, clicking their fingers—and talking, (clickings) walking Mrs. Lyons out of the door.

'Get lost!' said Beverley, '*Get lost!*'

Mrs. Lyons ran out in a fury. 'I've got to set a trap for these children.' The next day it was Thursday and . . . and they had to—the boys had to go up the field and girls had sewing. Yes! they did sewing all right! Sticking the pins up each other's bottoms. It wasn't very nice for Beverley Hall because you see: . . . well—she sort of landed headfirst in the clay pot—so—Mrs. Lyons came in—'STOP—THIS—NOISE!' she said.

'Ah, get lost!' said Beverley, 'Can't ee leave us alone once in a while, us good little girls?'

'Oh, impertinent little girls!' she said and ran out in a fury.

The next day the boys were back again. Beverley had invited all the class to tea. I don't know what her brother thought but—she invited them. Then after tea they went into her bedroom and played ghosties but unfortunately Michael Brock and Alan Masling, Clifford Luggar and Michael Perrot all fell off the bed and—er—Clifford Luggar bumped his head on the pottie so we had to go home.

Then the next day Mrs. Lyons came in expecting all the people—all the children to be roaring—but the children were as nice as sixpence. 'Good morning,' said everybody. 'Shall we get on with our maths?' Mrs. Lyons unfortunately fainted but I think she's recovered now, and that is the end of the story.

This improvised spoken story—with real characters and a real context known to everyone listening but the events fantastic and surprising—is in many ways very like Ruth Manning Saunders's folk tale about the boy who had to learn fear. It is told in a similar homely way, and is jokey and daring. The teachers are outwitted by cunning and high spirits and collective action, but they are also part of the conspiracy as willing listeners.

It is, however, very different from the written stories (the children's own or other people's) because these are *individual* stories, and this spontaneous spoken storytelling is a shared or collective effort. The storyteller couldn't have done it without the audience being there to gasp or laugh—and to know the characters and how unlikely or fantastic it all was.

Much of children's talk to their teachers in primary schools consists of mini-stories, and much of adults' informal conversations everywhere consists of these same anecdotes—the tissue of little personal stories by which we open our lives to other people and enter into theirs. What is their function? Is it comparable to the function of the stories discussed hitherto in this article or are such anecdotes merely some kind of personal indulgence? We tend to think of personal anecdotes as impeding the expression of ideas in a conversation, or as unnecessary "asides." Clearly their function will be different in different circumstances and we are interested here in the use that children make of them—for children may use them differently from adults, that they may have a developmental function.

The following transcript of a tape made by Elizabeth Grugeon of four ten-year-old children from one of her classes discussing *by themselves* a poem called *Rock, our dog* by a schoolboy is worth reading carefully to see how much of the conversation consists of personal anecdotes and what they contribute to the topic being discussed—in short, what the anecdotes are "about" in the sense that we are asked what the stories were really about in the first paragraph of this article.

It is not possible to reproduce the whole four-and-a-half pages of the transcript, but the opening conversation is quite adequate to show what the talk was like, and to provide evidence for Mrs. Grugeon's suggestion that the continual reference to personal experience is the children's way of understanding and considering the poem, which is about a boy's grief at the death of his dog.

Rock, our dog

He's dead now.
He was put to sleep last night.

I was sad,
but I did not cry.

It was not the same
without him here
to prance and
nuzzle his head
into my arms.

Today we were going
to bury him
in the garden.
I helped dig the hole,
and then ran off.

Nicholas Hadfield

J: Um, let's go on to *Rock, our dog*
S: This one's a bit sad, isn't it?
A: Yeah.
L: It's a sad one.
J: I've got a dog called Pip and it makes me think whether he's going to die.
S: We've got a great big dog . . . it's an incredible nuisance.
M: Like the dog next door, it's ten now.
S: When our dog next door died . . .
J: Actually; shall I tell you what I'd do if it were my dog, I'd help dig the hole but I'd run off.
S: I like the verse um, the second verse.
M: 'It was not the same/without him here/to prance and/nuzzle his head into my arms.'
S: That's nice, that one.
L: Yeah. It feels as if he's very, you know.
S: A nice dog.
L: Very happy with you, and he's always comforting you and . . .
J: Pip does that, ooh I thought she was dead when she came home from her operation, she had her tongue hanging out of her mouth, it was horrible.
S: You know when a dog goes to the doctor's or something and it makes you feel, I hope it comes back all right.
J: Oh yes.
M: I think, if a dog hates going to the vet . . . they can remember, kind of thing.
J: It goes . . . even for two days when it went to have its operation, I felt, I was missing it ever such a lot.

S: Do you think it's best to have the animal die or have it put to sleep?

L: Put to sleep.

M: Put to sleep.

S: That all depends, if it's in pain.

J: When it's in pain, put to sleep, but if it's, you know just ordinary old, and it's not alarmed or anything, then keep it till it dies.

S: Mostly, when it gets old, it does have something wrong with it, when it gets old. Our dog does, is all white round the face now because it's ten.

L: Well, I go all, um I don't know what, um how to, um what to talk about in this poem because we we've never had a dog and um, I'm not fond of dogs and I've never had one and I hate dogs.

S: I've had a dog since I was born.

M: But my nana had a little poodle dog and he had to be put to sleep because it was going all dizzy.

S: I'll never forget when I was small, our dog got run over.

J: My, well, dad, well we went and just brought the dog home, we didn't know anything about it and, you know, he said, look and I just thought it was going to be . . . and mum didn't let me go straight in she just said, now tell me what dad's brought in there and I thought it was a rabbit because you saw its white legs going like that when I opened the door.

S: Puppies.

J: Carol says to dad, whatever did you bring that home for and she picks it up and says, Ah isn't it lovely (laughter). My uncle John he's got the brother to it.

S: They're awfully playful when they're puppies but . . .

L: They're a nuisance.

J: My uncle's got another Jack Russell because we've got three Jack Russells in our family.

S: Our labrador was dreadful to train. We haven't trained it properly now, anyway.

M: When Lassie had puppies, we kind of had to look after them because they were always coming through their fence into our garden.

J: Do you mean Lassie your next door neighbor's dog?

M: Yeah

J: What about the other one?

S: Well, when our dog had puppies, you know, she was quite old, we thought she might die, she had eight.

J: Eight puppies?

S: Yes.

M: Lassie had ten.

L: What put mummy off . . .

J: Our dog's only a little one and he had four, two brown and two black and she's only a small dog really.

L: What put my mum off was that when they're first puppies, when they're first puppies, that's what put my mum off and hearing about all these alsatians mauling children. Mum says whenever you see a dog and it looks a bit vicious, just walk by normal, don't look scared, so whenever I go past Davies's I go walking along ... (laughter) they've got a great big alsatian, it goes (dog noises).

M: It's quite a nice dog.

L: No it wasn't, no it wasn't, um, they had two dogs and Freddy bought one of them, honestly ...

J: I think alsatians, oh they're horrible, they get on my nerves.

S: They're not.

L: I feel as if I'm going to get mauled any minute.

S: My sister, she's not frightened of dogs at all. She goes by every dog. She strokes it on its head and ...

J: So do I.

S: Mummy tries to say, you mustn't do that in case it bites you and one day she stroked this little poodle on top of its head and it went and bit her right on the hand. It didn't hurt her though, but she still does it. We've got a puppy down the road ...

J: Well Mr., his dog's rather blind actually, you know, it's got one eye blind and it's got all white and he says he has great fun watching Pip, because Pip gets (?) and she runs all the way on top I never thought of anything like her dying or anything, you just don't think of it.

S: There's a lovely labrador puppy down the bottom of our road now. Well it's only, they only had it for about a week or two weeks. It's gorgeous, it's called Tina.

J: When they're puppies ...

S: And it runs around trying to bite your heels, it's lovely.

M: ... an alsation called Tina, and she was ever such a nice doggy, she hadn't seen me at all before.

L: Doggy!

M: You know, she was ever so friendly.

J: But when you go up to dogs you don't think they're going to end up dying and you're going to end up crying and that, some dogs ...

S: I thought it was rather sad, when, um, Patch in *Blue Peter* dies.

A: Oh yes.

J: You've been with them all the time

L: Poor John. No?, which one was it?

S: It is John.

J: John.

L: Yeah, he er trained her and everything.

J: They still got . . .

S: It's a funny beginning in this poem.

J: They've still got Patch and the other dog.

S: He's dead now.

L: Let's go back to the poem.

M: Yes, well we're talking about the poem, we're talking about dogs.

L: Well, why did he say he's dead now? Why couldn't they start with he's dead?

S: Our dog . . . our dog's just died. That sounds better.

L: . . . than saying 'He's dead now'.

S: You could start "Our dog's just died, he was put to sleep last night." That sounds a little better.

M: Sounds kind of, more as if . . .

S: than "he's dead" . . .

M: . . . more as if he knows the dog . . .

J: . . . no, you get the feeling of it though, "He's dead now/He was put to sleep last night/I was sad/but I did not cry," but I would, I would cry my eyes out if my dog had just died.

L: Yeah, it's probably a boy though, isn't it, it's a boy who wrote it though?

S: Boys don't really seem to cry . . .

L: Boys don't cry very much, not as . . .

M: Not over that sort of thing . . .

L: They don't, not really, the girls are more sentimental and a bit more soppy.

S: No they're not.

M: Some boys are like that, specially if they've known it for a long time.

J: I helped dig a hole, I helped dig the hole and then ran off, and then ran off . . .

L: Oh I wouldn't.

S: I suppose he just ran off because he didn't want to see the dog being put into the um . . .

L: grave

S: grave

J: Yeah.

L: There's the, um, Sizes down the road and they had a dog and it's blind and they, and when it started howling when they were away, and it died, it was dead when they got back and they buried it under their, their favorite apple tree and they've got it smothered with flowers. It looked ever so pretty.

The children's anecdotes in this excerpt are about dogs dying, being ill or injured and growing old, in short about the death and birth and aging of animals. Occasionally they express explicitly the general idea that lies behind the anecdotes—for instance, Judy says: "When you go up to dogs you don't think they're going to end up dying and you're going to end up crying," but usually the general ideas are implicit and the discussion is carried along by the personal "stories," which also, of course, carry the feelings which the poem and the talk are primarily about. Linda, who is frightened of dogs, puts the whole thing in a nutshell when she says: "I don't know what, um how to, um what to talk about in this poem because we, we've never had a dog and um, I'm not fond of dogs and I've never had one and I hate dogs."

We suggest that the personal "stories" are in fact the basic fabric of children's conversations, the *means* by which they enter into other people's experiences, try them on for fit and advance into general ideas. It would seem likely that adults also do this, that we, collectively, through anecdotes, build up a shared representation of some aspect of life comparable in function to the view of life presented by a single narrator, or for example, the poem *"Bedtime,"* or the story of the boy who had to learn fear.

Linda was at first the odd man out: she disliked dogs and made the others recognize that dogs can be fierce or dangerous, but since the talk was really about the death of pets, and grief, she entered into it at a higher level of generality in her last contribution (in the excerpt) about the dog that was buried under the apple tree—and all this movement of ideas was by means of highly relevant anecdotes from personal experience.

Do these anecdotes belong to the discourse of storytelling? We suggest they do in that their function is similar to stories told by a single narrator, in this case a collective bringing together of their various experiences in order to explore and order these disturbing general ideas. The children who wrote *Bedtime* and *My story*, for instance, were also re-shaping their experiences, but in the case of the single narrator the representation was not subject to immediate modification by others, and could therefore be more coherent, more formally shaped and less direct. It might also therefore be about things that the writer could not, or did not want to, express directly, and the symbolic nature of the characters and events in the traditional stories gave them models for saying implicitly things that could not be said explicitly. But the obverse was also significant: the fact that at any moment in the talk someone might modify or oppose what one child had said gave talk in a group the possibility of moving more explicitly into general ideas. The pattern of talk in this excerpt shows clearly this shuttling movement between general ideas and personal anecdotes which illustrate, modify or advance the ideas.

At first sight this transcript appears as a gossipy piece of children's chat, but as one studies it, it comes into focus like a slide under a microscope, and we can begin to see this talk as a learning process wherein personal experiences are brought alongside the clearly envisaged circumstances of the boy's grief for his dog, and all sorts of possibilities considered about the lives and deaths of pets. One can also see in this passage of spoken discourse the way in which one is continually a spectator (through listening, or telling) of one's own and other people's lives, and that this whole universe of story, in all its manifestations, is what literature is.

References

Walter Benjamin. "The Storyteller," in *Illuminations.* Fontana, 1970.

Nancy Martin. "What Are They Up To?" in A. Jones and J. Mulford (eds) *Children Using Language: A New Approach to Language in the Primary School.* Oxford University Press, 1972.

Acknowledgments

Henrietta Dombey, Heather Lyons, and Sarah Evans, Head of Newton Hall Nursery, Framlingate Moor, County Durham.

4

Children Writing Poetry

In a sense poems are "plays": response to literature is a kind of reply to the writer speaking to you, so that the reader engages in a dialogue, but young children cannot enter into this kind of dialogue. Their speech, and therefore their thought, is still so much a part of a physical situation that they need a full dramatic "representation" to embody their complex thoughts and feelings. Susan Isaacs tells of the play of the "poor lost child," who had been invited by the taxi-men to go for a drive. When they were a hundred miles from home they asked her to pay her fare. She had no money, and they turned her out in the middle of the road. She then wandered about until she was tired and lay down in the middle of the road and slept. Her mother had to go and look for her all through Kensington Gardens. The taxi-men sent her the wrong way when she asked where her little girl was; but in the end she found her. This example of dramatic play, improvised co-operatively, expresses anxieties and a final reassurance which could never be expressed in talk because children's language is not sufficiently explicit to formulate such notions. Hopes and fears, premonitions and aspirations can only be given shape in symbolic *representations* such as this one; but dramatic play is not the only form that children use. Drawing and painting serve the same end—and writing, once they can write.

And what they write is, at first, not differentiated, or differentiable, into prose and poetry. Take this, for instance, by a nine-year-old boy:

The Funeral

On the hills I saw a funeral and two men were carrying a coffin. The people behind were relatives of the dead person. Nearby was a fire.

First published in *Presenting Poetry: A Handbook for English Teachers*, Thomas Blackburn (ed.), Methuen for the University of London Institute of Education, 1966.

They were going to throw the coffin on the fire. A priest said a prayer and a lady broke down and wept as the coffin hit the fire. Thick black smoke filled the sky then everyone who was there wept. They stayed there until the fire blew out. Then everyone except the lady walked sadly away. The lady didn't go with the others, she stayed and wept. Slowly she rose from the ground and mourned for whoever was dead. I went across to see if any other person was around but no one was there. The hills were dark and empty and the sun was sinking slowly. I ran after the others and told them to come back, but only one came, that was a little boy. He was about four but he could run fast. The lady smiled a little when she saw the little boy. They walked together along the dark hills.

No one who does not know the writer can say what this is really about, what it represents; but we can say that in writing it, he has "socialized" it, has built some sort of bridge between his fantasy and the real world.

As children grow older in the Junior School, poems and stories become more differentiated and they begin to have a sense of words as things to play with. They like to listen to rhymes and to repeat them, and, where they can, to modify the ones they know, and improvise others. So they see poems as "games"—similar to, and perhaps the same as, the game they play in a ring as they sing:

Poor Jennie is a-weeping, a-weeping, a-weeping,
Poor Jennie is a-weeping on a bright summer's day . . .

It is at this point that one can perceive two directions in their writing—themes and games. Their themes explore the regions of their daily life and their imaginative wanderings. Here is one from daily life by a boy of six:

Yesterday I watched a man with a compressor, and he let me dig with it, and my sister couldn't believe it. Only I really did work it. They have dug it all up now, and they have filled some of it in. They had made a man-hole. But they haven't filled that in yet. Because it is not finished yet. They have got a tractor, and, I like watching them working. I had some super fun yesterday. With all Wednesday off. With my old clothes on and my boots. Clumping about in the mud, and watching the men. The best man I liked was the man who drived the tractor. Because he let me drive the compressor. It was good driving the compressor. They have dug all the road up. Nobody can get through except me.

But sometimes the themes are recurrent, like the series of pictures that a seven-year-old girl painted when her mother was in hospital having a second baby. These were all pictures of a beautiful mother holding a baby.

It is the themes in children's writing that are important, and if, at this age, they try to treat their themes as games and use rhymes and marked rhythms and stanza-forms, they destroy the symbolic themes which are the mainspring of their writing. Their control of language is not good enough to incorporate what they really want to say into formal patterns, so the rhymes take control and produce, on the whole, trivial writing in which the sound dictates the sense. Tolstoi recalls how when he was a child of eight or nine the idea occurred to him to write some verses to present to his grandmother on her name-day and he immediately made up two verses with rhymes hoping to do the rest just as easily, but found, try as he would, he could not produce any more. In searching through his tutor's books he found a poem which attracted him "by the touching feeling with which it was imbued," so he learned it by heart and took it as a model and composed twelve lines in this manner, but in copying out his poem which had seemed wholly satisfactory to him, he found he was disturbed by the last line:

And love thee like our own dear mother.

He grew more and more dissatisfied with this line because it seemed disloyal to his mother; he could not love any one else as he loved her; but he was bound by the rhymes, and was unable to alter it, so presented it as it was. His grandmother was delighted with his gift, but he asked himself "Why had I written a lie?" His poem began as a "game," but since a mother is inevitably a "theme," it took him into deeper water than he had expected.

Miss Doolan, speaking about her Listening and Writing series in the B.B.C. Schools Broadcasting Service, said: "I want the pieces to come out of the loudspeaker, into the ears of the child, then sink down and stimulate reaction from the accumulated experiences there that will spark off a new piece of writing; not a copy, but the child's own. The poems the children write are the instinctive response of their own consciousness; for writing, to be true, must reflect the life and nature of the writer, a child's life and nature, and for this reason must be regarded as a professional job."

These sunken experiences, and their attendant emotions, are one of the main sources of literature, for children no less than for established writers. In his autobiography Edwin Muir wrote:

My height from the ground determined my response to other things too. When my father and Sutherland brought in the horses from the fields I stood trembling among their legs, seeing only their great, bearded feet and the momentary flash of their crescent-shaped shoes flung up lazily as they passed. When my father stopped with the bridle in his hands to speak to me I stood looking up at the stationary hulks and the tossing heads, which in the winter dusk were lost in the sky. I felt beaten down by an enormous weight and a real terror; yet I did not hate the horses as I hated the insects; my fear turned into something else, for it was infused by a longing to go up to them and touch them and simultaneously checked by the knowledge that their hoofs were dangerous: a combination of emotions which added up to worship in the Old Testament sense. Everything about them, the steam rising from their soft, leathery nostrils, the sweat staining their hides, their ponderous, irresistible motion, the distant rolling of their eyes, which was like the revolution of rock-crystal suns, the waterfall sweep of their manes, the ruthless flick of their cropped tails, the plunge of their iron-shod hoofs striking fire from the flagstones, filled me with a stationary terror and delight for which I could get no relief.

He also wrote this poem about the threat of atomic war.

The Horses

Barely a twelvemonth after
The seven days war that put the world to sleep,
Late in the evening the strange horses came.
By then we had made our covenant with silence,
But in the first few days it was so still
We listened to our breathing and were afraid.
On the second day
The radios failed; we turned the knobs; no answer.
On the third day a warship passed us, heading north,
Dead bodies piled on the deck. On the sixth day
A plane plunged over us into the sea. Thereafter
Nothing. The radios dumb;
And still they stand in corners of our kitchens,
And stand, perhaps, turned on, in a million rooms
All over the world. But now if they should speak,
If on a sudden they should speak again,
If on the stroke of noon a voice should speak,
We would not listen, we would not let it bring
That old bad world that swallowed its children quick
At one great gulp. We would not have it again.
Sometimes we think of the nations lying asleep,
Curled blindly in impenetrable sorrow,
And then the thought confounds us with its strangeness.

The tractors lie about our fields; at evening
They look like dank sea-monsters couched and waiting.
We leave them where they are and let them rust:
"They'll moulder away and be like other loam."
We make our oxen drag our rusty ploughs,

Long laid aside. We have gone back
Far past our fathers' land.

And then, that evening
Late in the summer the strange horses came.
We heard a distant tapping on the road,
A deepening drumming; it stopped, went on again
And at the corner changed to hollow thunder.
We saw the heads
Like a wild wave charging and were afraid.
We had sold our horses in our fathers' time
To buy new tractors. Now they were strange to us
As fabulous steeds set on an ancient shield
Or illustrations in a book of knights.
We did not dare go near them. Yet they waited,
Stubborn and shy, as if they had been sent
By an old command to find our whereabouts
And that long-lost archaic companionship.
In the first moment we had never a thought
That they were creatures to be owned and used.
Among them were some half-a-dozen colts
Dropped in some wilderness of the broken world,
Yet new as if they had come from their own Eden.
Since then they have pulled our ploughs and borne our loads,
But that free servitude still can pierce our hearts.
Our life is changed; their coming our beginning.*

It is the source which is being tapped when children improvise such themes for dramatic play as "the poor lost child." It recurs in the themes children use in order to dramatize in writing their current preoccupations, just as Edwin Muir's earliest feelings about the great farm horses are interwoven as symbols into his poem.

Sometimes children's writings celebrate happy experiences, such as the piece about the compressor; sometimes they represent disturbing ones, and this representation may go some way towards exorcising the anxiety or grief. Here is such a piece of writing by a twelve-year-old boy:

Take It Back

Take it back
He said in
A reluctant voice
Which didn't understand.

---

* Edwin Muir, *Collected Poems*, Faber and Faber.

Harsh and firm
Which didn't understand
The need for such a trivial thing
Needed by mother and child.

The thing was small
The need was big
But their need wasn't noticed.

Things like this
Had to go and so it went.
The cold weather outside
Was as bad as taking it back.

Cold and wet
Like winter
It blended in
With the sorrow.

They knocked
There was no reply
The boy leaned on the door
And it opened.

They looked at each
Other and understood
Each other and
They laid it inside.

Celebration and exorcism are probably the most important purposes (unconscious) in children's poems, but in between there is all that welter of descriptive writing and the "word games." Here is a descriptive piece:

Christmas Landscape

The stars glow brightly in the sky.
You see the patterns your breath makes in the air.
The snow lies on the land, crunching underfoot.
And then the Lord was born.

Here is a "word game":

Poems

Goddard and I
Are poem writers.
We write poems
Short and long.
We are making a book

In which to put them
In the month of May.
We have twenty poems completed
Short are mine I must say.

All these forms serve the writers' purposes.

If Miss Doolan is right when she says children's writing should be regarded as a professional job, then there are implications as to how teachers should try to get children writing, and how they should receive what is written. We should try to get children to write their *own* writing, marked with their own identity and out of their own inner and outer life, at their own varying levels, sincerely and with truth. We should not try to impose techniques, but free the channels for the imagination to impose its own forms on the writing. If children have been used to talking about everything and to hearing and reading stories and poems, the forms and language patterns of these will be in their inner ears, and will be used in the representations they make when they write. An eight-year-old girl began a story thus:

> Once on a cold moor which was covered with gorse and purple heather there lived a horrible witch . . .

The classic form of storytelling lies behind her opening sentence but at eight years old one has no conscious literary art. So critical comments are not only a waste of time, but an active disturbance, and marks would also seem to be irrelevant if one assumes that each child is writing in his own way for his own purposes.

But children do want someone to read what they have written and to talk to them about it—about its content, not about its form; and if they can maintain the confidence acquired in good Junior Schools, that anything that is important or interesting to them will be so regarded by their teacher, all the resources of their inner and outer experience are available and there need be no more searching for subjects.

The question of what a teacher does with what children write is of particular importance in the Secondary School because nearly all the currents of Secondary education run counter to the development of imaginative and personal writing.

The organization of the schools is such that there are different teachers for every subject and most of these subjects—as they are taught—employ formal uses of English which exlcude the personal view and are quite unlike talk, or childish thought. Furthermore, examination syllabuses tend to reach right down into the lower forms of Secondary Schools so that there is both recognized and unrecognized pressure for pupils to develop the modes of impersonal language which are necessary for all-round educational advance. They must master these modes if they are to master the content of the syllabuses in the various subjects. This means that the main part of the children's formal learning experiences is in a language which excludes individual interpretations of those experiences. Imaginative writing, and particularly writing poems, acts as some sort of counter-balance to the increasing formalism of their other work. While, for more able pupils, the work can provide considerable intellectual stimulus, it can leave it unconnected, as it were, to their own deeper personal lives; the less able pupils are, on the whole, too discouraged and confused to enter into these areas of learning in any way that is significant for them. Here is a poem by a second-year girl on this subject:

The Fool of the Class

I hate my teacher
He made me the fool of the class,
Making me try to explain
About things I don't know,
What a fool he made me look.

Look at them laughing
And saying I'm a fool
They'll never let me forget it
Never at all
About the time he made me a fool.

Explain it he said
Explain it please
But I don't know how to
You don't indeed
Disgraceful, disgraceful
He muttered aloud.

Then there is the continuous pressure to get things right, as distinct from wrong. Clearly this is important in most of the learning the children do in subjects other than English and Art, but there is a tendency for both pupils and teachers to transfer these same notions of right and wrong to literature and to their own writing where they are not appropriate. This makes children lose confidence in using language in their own way.

But one is usually free to write a poem as one pleases. Most teachers will not "correct" poems in the way they feel it necessary to correct prose, so writing a poem gives a *sense* of freedom from the rules of language, and such a sense is the starting point of creative uses of language. Furthermore, poems are usually short and intense in feeling, and they are more like talk than is most prose, so in all these ways they are particularly appropriate to young and immature writers, and particularly valuable in the Secondary

School, because they provide the link between children's own uses of language and those of adult literature.

But poetry can take one into deep waters, deeper than adolescent children often want to go, and in the third year at Secondary School there is sometimes a reaction away from the commitment of writing poems that are "true reflections of one's nature and life." Stories or satires may be more satisfactory forms of writing at this age, or studies and investigations of a more detached kind. A year or two later "themes" reappear, in that they want to write on subjects which draw on their imaginative and reflective inner lives and these will often be matters of equal concern to adults. Here contemporary poets are of the utmost importance, and the poems the children read and the poems they write can provide an oasis of personal interpretation of experience which is much needed in the fragmentation of learning which our Secondary system presupposes.

5

The Place of Literature in the "Universe of Discourse"

If we survey the English teaching scene since Dartmouth we can see that we have got quite a long way in redefining English as a mother tongue. We understand it is for use—and is learnt by use rather than by precept. But we haven't got all that far in understanding the place of literature in this "universe of discourse" as James Moffett called it. The members of the Dartmouth Seminar were quite clear about it: "Literature is a significant part of personal experience and can therefore be as much a part of a reader's experience as events in his own life" and, as John Dixon reports, can illuminate and extend the language activities of the English classroom. Yet, in the pedagogical writing about English teaching since Dartmouth, a myth has grown up that the "growth model" of English takes no account of literature. Barry Smith, in an article as recently as 1977 (Eagleson and Watson, 1977), could write:

> Is an English teacher a person who works with poems, stories, novels and plays, or is he concerned primarily with promoting talking, writing and reading about the students' direct experiences and other areas of interest?
>
> The "experience" approach assumes that the focal point of Subject English is language in all its uses and contexts with the activities of talking, reading and writing about topics which interest the students taking precedence over the provision of literary experience. Literary experience is relegated to the background as one of the "voices" contributing to the "conversation" in the classroom. In a very radical approach, literature would hardly matter at all.

Published in *The Martin Report: What Goes On in English Lessons*, Case Studies from Government High Schools, Western Australia, Department of Education, W. A., 1980.

It is curious that the part of the Dartmouth program which deals with talk and with the personal uses of language has been fairly widely assimilated into the vanguard of classroom practice and theory, whereas that part which articulates the notion of a universe of discourse in which one of the uses of language is literature—and a highly significant use—has not been assimilated; it has, in fact, been quite overlooked, so that many people think it isn't there. It is as if people feel a necessity to maintain the separateness of the two "disciplines," language and literature, and therefore refuse to recognize that there is, in fact, a universe of discourse. After all, literature is an artifact constructed from language, and a highly significant use of it.

Why is there this curious blind spot?

Partly it turns on the meaning people have come to give to the word *experience.* Literary experience seems to be excluded from the connotation of the word, yet quite young students do not so exclude it, as the following quotation from the journal of a thirteen-year-old girl in one of our case studies shows:

> June 2nd. My poem, "In the Days of the Ring," does not exactly tell a story. I know why I wrote it. In a way I was trying to fathom how I felt about the book, "The Lord of the Rings." I also ask the questions I want to ask about it. I wish to see Galadriel and like this I also want to say what I want to hear about more—to know "Where have all my dear friends gone?"—but are they my dear friends? In terms of reality they are nothing. They are just J.R. Tolkien's children.

In part, the refusal to see literary experience as a part of all experience is a product of the way literature is taught in universities and therefore in schools in preparation for the examinations leading up to university entrance. The focus is on a training in discrimination and literary criticism, university teachers themselves having a heavy investment in critical studies. John Dixon wrote (Dixon, 1967):

> While the Seminar (which was very largely composed of university teachers) was united in the essential value of literary experiences . . . it was full of doubt and dismay about prevailing approaches to the teaching of literature, not only at school level. . . . It is literature, not literary criticism, which is the subject.

But the problem is broader than this. We are still entangled in a view of literature as something "out there" that other people write. This puts the focus on a "trained elite" who aim to distinguish even among contemporary writers those who will "last;" i.e. literature is seen as something that *has been.*

There is an alternative view which has been growing in recent years.

It is a view which has arisen from studies of the various functions of language within the whole universe of discourse. James Britton develops this view and explores its implications in Chapter III of *Language and Learning.* (Britton, 1970) From this stance one of the uses (or functions) of language is to make (create) "literature," and it can be seen to be a universal activity, not the prerogative of a few. To exemplify: everyone tells mini-stories of their own and other people's lives; many people read stories—newspapers are full of them; and millions of people watch stories on TV. Thus within the universe of discourse one can say that all story-makers and all story consumers are engaged in the same *kind* of operation, and are using language (and other means) for a similar purpose. "Narrative," says Barbara Hardy, "is a primary act of mind transferred to Art from Life." (Hardy, 1977) This is *not* to say that all stories are equally valuable. This is where experience of reading and discrimination come in, but they come in on a broader scenario in which a student's writing appears as of the same *kind* as that of an established writer, although its quality may be very different. And it needs to be recognized that in the contemporary world the medium of literature is not only print but also TV and film.

Of course, the functions of literature itself are various. Much that is written (and read and watched) are collective day-dreams and satisfy because they confirm current attitudes and beliefs. Other writing provides fantasy worlds which keep the real world at bay for a time; and yet other writing genuinely explores the boundaries of human behavior and enlarges our understanding of the possibilities of life. Inevitably we see the third kind of writing as being superior, and there is a real place for criticism in attempting to see which writers are doing what (and which writers are not doing any of these things but using writing to serve non-literary ends such as advertising or pornography). Perhaps new critics considering literature in its role in society may be able to recognize these various functions of literature and see their relationship to human needs.

A number of writers have explored a functional view of literature. D. W. Harding in *The Role of the Onlooker* (1936) and *Psychological Processes in the Reading of Fiction* (1962) considers the social function of literature; James Britton developed the idea of the significance in a person's life of the role of the "spectator"—in short, of literature; and James Moffett in *Teaching the Universe of Discourse* has powerful things to say about the nature of writing in the "mythic" mode as distinct from the expository mode, especially for children.

It is surely time we began to pay more attention to these (and other) writers and to explore the implications of what they say for the place of literature in schools. It seems as if the fact that they have dared to place literature within a context of language as a whole has made us deaf to what they are saying about the universality and centrality of literature.

Response to Literature

For many years the notion of the "right response" has dominated literature teaching. This, of course, is first cousin to "getting the answer right" in other subjects. "The right response" includes not only "right" meanings but also preferring those works at the top of the hierarchy. This view of response ignores the active, creative power which is naturally as much a part of the process of reading as it is of writing. We have noted that in writing in schools this active, creative power is beginning to be recognized, but in reading it is still straight-jacketed by the notion that there is a one-to-one relationship between the quality of the literature and the reader's response to it. This is an over-simple, mechanistic view. In fact, as we can learn from tape recordings of students discussing poems and stories, or from what they occasionally write about them, they can bring empathy, sensitivity and relevant experience to bear on all sorts of literary items—good, bad and indifferent—which are transformed by active creative power into items of significance for them. To illustrate, here is a quotation from a boy of twelve writing about poems that he liked:

> What a picture I get from the second last verse of Robert Southey's poem "The Inchape Rock." Sir Ralph the Rover is sailing home with a ship full of treasure with no thought of danger now that his perilous voyage is over when suddenly,
>
>> They hear no sound, the swell is strong;
>> Though the wind hath fallen they drift along,
>> Till the vessel strikes with a shivering shock,
>> "O Christ it is the Inchape Rock."
>
> No prose could express so well the anguish of the man who knew he was doomed and by his own folly in removing the warning bell from the rock. That verse shows me him tearing his hair, running frantically up and down giving orders, but it is to no avail and his ship sinks slowly but surely until at last only the bow sticks out of the water. Then even that disappears and only a few bubbles remain on the surface.

Surely we would not dismiss this response as spurious because we might be inclined to dismiss Southey's ballad as spurious? To quote James Britton again: "These unsophisticated responses are the stuff from which, with refinement and development, literary responses are made." (Britton, 1968) We may expect children's tastes to broaden with experience of reading; what seems to be needed is joint negotiation of what is read in school, and mutual respect for differing tastes.

Literature in Integrated Studies

Part of the core curriculum that schools provide is in humanities, more often called social studies. Broadly, this study is concerned with man in his physical and cultural environment, past and present. If we think in terms of separate disciplines—or subjects—this means geography, English, history, and sometimes sociology and philosophy. Since school systems are dominated by matter to be learned for examinations, the notion of the educative value of the humanities is little more than a wraith hovering behind the programs. Few will see history either as the march of progress or (as Gibbon saw it) "as a register of the crimes and follies and misfortunes of mankind"; or literature as a transmitter of cultural values through its imagined representations of the possibilities of life. Yet here and there it does work in this way.

An upper school student responding to an invitation from the London Writing Research team to reflect on the way he writes in his two main subjects, English and history, said:

> The two main subjects for which I write are History and English Literature. I enjoy English more as a subject, but I find writing for History somewhat easier. English essays demand an organization of ideas which is also necessary in History, but the difference is that ideas in English often have to do with verbalizing feelings, while History essays deal with what you think. English demands a rigorous examination of your own reaction to a novel or poem, while in History the difficulty is not so much the formulation of ideas as the marshalling of facts, and the clarification of notions which you had all along. It is because English is more to do with the non-cerebral part of your mind that it is more difficult to write about and more satisfying at the same time. History essays may be slightly easier (though often the marshalling of facts is just drudgery), but they are less satisfying, indeed, the age-old story of human failure is often downright depressing ... the sense of achievement (in English essays) is greater because the transference of ideas from the inexplicit (or implicit) to the explicit, intellectual, and cerebral part of the mind is such a difficult, and time-consuming process. (Quoted in Dixon and Gill, 1977)

It is one of the intentions of integrated programs that the different fields of study should illuminate each other in the way they have for this student, but there are special problems for English in these combined studies, and much confusion.

To identify these problems: firstly, English is the medium in which other subjects are conducted so the practical matters of reading and writing in these studies is—quite rightly—seen as an aspect of English which is fulfilled "across the curriculum." But this is not the sum total of English, though it is often thought to be so by students, parents and many teachers. One student said in an interview, "We don't do English anymore; we do social studies." The use of English to articulate a field of public knowledge (social studies) is only one of its functions. There is also the whole area of a student's response to broader aspects of experience—aspects that belong to his life as an individual and that should find expression in views he may hold, in poems he may write, or events he may feel moved to reflect on. These can't be predicted or provided for within the syllabus of a set program, and are therefore a particular responsibility of teachers of English. What happens (often) to these uses of language within the social studies framework? Regrettably they are lost, and their loss diminishes a significant area of personal growth.

Writing is important for the articulation of personal as well as public knowledge. To quote from our case studies, a 17-year-old student said:

> I often used my writing as a thought-formulating process. . . . It helped me to understand myself and my place in life. . . . In a very indirect way this better understanding of myself helped me to develop an identity and gain confidence in myself as an individual.

And another said.

> . . . The most outstanding value gained for me was that I became more aware of the outside world.

Two documentations from students of the importance to them of personal writing—but how do they fit into a social studies program?

Secondly, there is the question of literature. Within the social studies framework literature tends to be selected for its usefulness in illustrating something else, i.e. the topics of the course. Moreover, these illustrations are, too often, short excerpts pulled out of stories or novels or even poems. Such extracts can be illuminating; they are usually better written than textbooks, but in the context of integrated programs they are deficient—and dangerous—in regard to literature because they come to be regarded by teachers as fulfilling the literature component in the program, and by students as being chunks of social studies reading matter—which is, in fact, what they have become. A story is an end in itself; when it is made to serve some other end, its function changes.

Furthermore, the form of a work of literature is part of its meaning. Excerpts inevitably diminish its meaning, and when used as illustrations of something else, may distort or destroy its essence. For instance, the verse of Southey's poem quoted above in the context of an argument makes a telling point in the argument, but it gives us no experience of the poem.

Even when circumstances are more favorable—when, for instance, all the teachers in a humanities course plan a program which includes whole works of literature relevant to the program—there is still some loss in literary experience, though the English teachers may consider that this loss is compensated for by the gains of an integrated course. This loss is to do with the unpredictability of how literature works for people. The power of stories and poems to "speak" to people lies partly in how they relate here and now to aspects of individual lives. Texts chosen in accordance with a social studies course may or may not work in this way. If they do, it is probably a happy accident, since the destinations and starting points are different. A social studies course starts from a designated *topic;* English teachers set about choosing books in all sorts of ways, but apart from constraints such as prescribed texts or the availability of books in the school, it is probably true to say that their starting point is likely to be the particular *students* they are planning for. They think about such things as the levels of maturity of their students, their experience of reading and to some extent their individual tastes. Sometimes they think students ought to encounter some of the work of a particular writer; sometimes they discuss with their students what writers or what books they would like to read; sometimes they too start from a topic, but particularly, many English teachers try to keep open the ways in which literature can interact with daily life. To take an unusually dramatic example, Gwyn came into his primary school one day and said to his teacher, "Me cat died, Miss. Can you help me find a story about a cat, Miss? When you read something it helps you sort it out in your mind." (Martin, 1976) These various ways of selecting literature will not fit easily into a social studies program.

Then there is the matter of a different destination. The purpose of literature in a social studies course is necessarily didactic, to illuminate a topic in some way. Literature has no such transactional purpose:

> For poetry makes nothing happen; it survives
> In the valley of its saying where executives
> Would never want to tamper. (Auden, 1950)

Yet all these problems could be overcome if the different nature of the different humanities was recognized. *Ad hoc* arrangements can be legislated for. The problem lies more in the confusion about the multiple roles of English—maid of all work, instrument of thought, creator of works of imagination. Because of its scope it is the core of the humanities, but it needs to be given that scope; and since its handmaidenly and instrumental roles are included in the other humanities, literature (and its corollary, personal writing) is the unique contribution of subject English. It may be possible for students to say they don't do English in such a program; it should not be possible for them to say they don't do literature.

III

Language
Across the Curriculum:
Writing and Learning—
A Potential for Change

Over the decade 1966–76 the British Schools Council funded two major writing projects at London University Institute of Education. The first (1966–72) was a research enquiry into the development of writing abilities, 11 to 18 years, under the direction of James Britton. This team envisaged writing as shaped by thinking, and as changing under the influence of who and what it was written for. The second (1971–76) was a development project (*Writing Across the Curriculum 11 to 16*) under the direction of Nancy Martin, set up to disseminate the theory and findings of the Writing Research team referred to above. It was also charged with working in schools to explore with teachers of all subjects the implications of the Writing Research findings for learning across the curriculum.

In "What Are They Up To?" the Writing Research models of discourse were used to examine what children seem to be doing when they write. The study undermines old assumptions about how to promote children's basic language skills and shows that the extent to which children meaningfully represent their world will depend on how much opportunity they are given to write expressively; and the power of imaginative writing to generate language and to bring complex thoughts and feelings within a writer's grasp is clearly shown. Good transactional writing, on the other hand, is hard to find in any quantity in schools. The Project team set out to track it down and identify the kinds of classroom environments where it seemed to flourish.

49

6

The Writing Research Models of Discourse:

Function and A Sense of Audience

The Writing Research team (Britton et al. 1975) funded by the Schools Council to investigate the development of writing abilities at the secondary level was faced with what was essentially the same problem as teachers in schools attempting to look at the language their pupils encounter and use across the curriculum; they asked themselves the same questions: What kinds of language should pupils have opportunities to use? and does it matter if they don't? Are some kinds more important than others to the pupils' learning? Are some kinds more difficult to acquire? What are the circumstances most favorable to children acquiring them?

A first step in attempting to answer such questions was to survey a wide sample of school writing (2,000 scripts). To do this and to describe them, we developed a model of mature written discourse. We assumed that the socializing effect of school would cause school writings to approximate—more or less—adult models, though we did not discount the possibility that we might find some writing which existed only in schools. This model allowed us to place each piece of student writing at some point on one of two scales; not scales of quality, but scales of (1) function and (2) a sense of audience—what the writing was for and who it was for. Though other dimensions might be examined, these we felt were of primary importance in affecting what and how the writer wrote. Models are developed for particular purposes and we were seeking one which would allow us to classify school writings by other categories than those of subject and thereby enable us to study the comparable intellectual problems which would be, we predicted, reflected in the writing from various subjects. These would be masked, as they are in practice today, if we viewed various kinds of writ-

Published in *Language Across the Curriculum*, M. Marland (ed.), Heinemann, 1977.

ing as being proper only to various subjects. We thought that intellectual growth transcended subject boundaries and that we should be able to trace this more generally by looking at kinds of writing across the curriculum, since verbal-mental operations such as report, explanation, argument, classification, comment, narrative, etc. are not peculiar to any one subject.

The Function Model

First, then, the Function model, designed to help us look at what writing is for. This is not exactly the same as a writer's purpose because our culture has itself developed distinct language forms which are typically associated with certain situations. We know quite well, for instance, when we are in a story, or a sermon, or being persuaded to buy something, because we have internalized these kinds of language from our day-to-day encounters with them. When children come to write in similar situations, they draw on their pool of language experience, which helps them to know what kind of language to use in certain types of situations. For instance, no one teaches children in an infant class to begin their stories "Once upon a time," or "Once there was a little pig . . .," but most of them do this because this beginning is so obviously a "marker" of stories which they have listened to or read.

The boundaries are by no means hard and fast, but it has been found possible and useful to distinguish three broad categories of function to which recognizably distinct kinds of writing belong. What distinguishes them is that writer and reader mutually recognize the conventions that distinguish one "job" from another. It is true that there are often linguistic differences but these are the markers of the different functions whose essential differences lies in the sort of things the writer takes for granted about his reader's responses. To take a simple example, if we read "Once upon a time there was a flying horse," we know the writer is taking it for granted that we recognize a story and will not quarrel about whether horses can fly.

Our model distinguishes three main "recognized and allowed for" functions of writing, *transactional, expressive* and *poetic.*

The Expressive Function

The central term of the model is taken from Edward Sapir (1961), who pointed out that ordinary face-to-face speech is directly expressive and carries out its referential function in close and complex relationship with that expressive function. Since much writing by young children is very like written down speech, we described the expressive function as that *in which it is taken for granted* that the writer himself is of interest to the reader; he feels free to jump from facts to speculations to personal anecdote to emotional outburst to reflective comment—as he wishes—and none of it will be used against him. It is all part of being a person *vis-à-vis* another person. It is the means by which the new is tentatively explored, thoughts may be half-uttered, attitudes half-expressed, the rest being left to be picked up by a listener or reader who is willing to take what is expressed in whatever form it comes, and the unexpressed on trust.

The Writing Research Team said: "The more we worked on this idea of the expressive function, the more important we felt it to be. Not only is it the mode in which we approach and relate to each other in speech, but it is also the mode in which, generally speaking, we frame tentative first drafts of new ideas. By analogy with these roles in speech, it seemed likely to us that expressive writing might play a key role in a child's learning. It must surely be the most accessible form in which to write, since conversation will have provided the writer with a familiar model. Furthermore, a writer who envisages his reader as someone with whom he is on *intimate* terms must surely have very favorable conditions for using the process of writing as a means of exploration and discovery" (Britton et al. 1975).

We quote in illustration three examples taken from metal-work, middle school science, and social studies which contain many of the features of expressive writing.

An excerpt from a long account of a project in metal-work by a boy of twelve.

The becoming of a gnat killer

the name Gnat Killer came to me after the project for maths I had been doing, you see I was going to do a project to see how many people spelt Gnat rong they ither spell it Kat, Gnate, Knate, Knatte, and even Knatt. well when I started to do my project, I thought well I will call it the Gnat then Killer came into my mind because I am mad on Horror. So I called it the Gnat Killer, it may sound violent but it isn't well at least I don't think, it is only another name been created to the world for the perpose of a project, I don't know if my turnin two the dictionary, it will read

> Gnat Killer
> name for
> a dagger used
> by Ricky Baker
> in 1972 8th dec:
> (not spelt nat killer)

that is only my idear thoe not that it will work.

The children watched an egg hatching in the science lab. They were asked to write about it in any way they liked. We quote two examples to show the variation in perceptions and focus.

The Chick Hatching (In the science lab).

The egg was begginning to crack, the chick inside was using all the strength it had to get out from being trapped inside the shell. I thought to myself, if just I could get a knife and crack the shell gently, then I could see what the chick look like. I kept seeing bits of the chicks wing as it was slowly cracking. The chick was gradually pushing it's way out, but could not go no further, because the other eggs were in the way, so our science teacher (Mr bowman) gently lifted the lid of the incubator and the egg that was cracking was moved away from the other eggs, Now the chick was not having such a struggle. you could see it pushing up against the top of the shell, and then going down for a rest. I said to Mr bowman will the chick be hatched by the time the bell goes, and mr bowman took it as a joke, put his head down on the incubator and said "will you be hatched by the time the bell goes." don't worry the chick did not reply.

The chick was just about hatched now, all it had to do was struggle out of the top of the shell, it was just about out, as it got out all the class shouted, "it's out!"

It was just standing up properly, with all it's feather's sticking up on end, it looked around in wonder, then the bell went and mr bowman put the lid back on the incubator.

"The Egg. . . ."

The egg begins to hatch, the crowd of children cluster around the humid inqubator. The egg cracks about 3cms, the egg tooth on the chick's beak can be spotted, the chick pants as he catches his first breath of fresh air then he goes back to work the egg opens about another centermeter then the chick lays back gasping for air it rests for about a minite then on it goes to crack the egg it pants and gasps catchies abreath then back to work in about ten minutes the egg is hatched the chick's feathers are wet and flat and the chick lays panting in about two minits time he is stood up then the feathers begin to dry off and fluff up then it becomes steaddy and soon enough it will be walking around.

An excerpt from a fourth-year boy's account of his work in social studies. Of his project on "The British political system" he writes:

This was the first big project I did and now when I look at it I marvel at how pathetic it is. . . . I have placed emphasis on the wrong things and made all the mistakes I was warned about . . . so it ended up in my eyes as a great failure. But I have learnt more from that project than any other piece of work I have ever done at school so it was only a failure in terms of what it was, not what was learnt from it. I learnt not only how to improve my work from this project but believe it or not I also learnt a great deal more than I already know about the British political system although most of it is not in the project.

These writings have many of the features that characterize speech—the utterances stay close to the speakers, reflecting the ebb and flow of thought and feeling, and like speech this expressive language is always on the move. It moves according to the demands of what it is for (all are towards the transactional in that they are giving information), what the reader wants to hear, and how the writer's language resources allow him to meet these demands—his own and other people's. All three would seem to have the self as audience and also their teacher, whom they believed when he told them to write as they wanted. In addition, Ricky Baker and the fourth-year boy had some vague sense of a wider audience in that they knew their writing was for someone at London University to read.

The Transactional Function

In transactional writing it is taken for granted that the writer means what he says and can be challenged for its truthfulness to public knowledge and its logicality; that it is sufficiently explicit and organized to stand on its own and does not derive its validity from coming from a particular person. So it is the typical language in which science and intellectual inquiry is *presented* to others (not necessarily the kind of language in which these activities are carried out); the typical language of transactions: technology, planning, reporting, instructing, informing, explaining, advising, arguing and theorizing—and, of course, the language most used in school writing. It can be more or less expressive, too, but the more familiar the writer is with the information or the arguments or whatever, the easier it is to respond to the demand of explicitness and the less the need for expressive features.

Ian was in the same metal-work class as Ricky. His project was a brass dish, and he wrote a long piece about brass and how you work it and how he made his dish; but, although there are expressive features in his writing, his purpose is firmly transactional. He feels himself to be knowledgeable about brass and sets out to *inform* his readers. The differences between his piece and Ricky's (quoted above) illustrate the differences between writing that is focused on a transaction and writing following the free flow of the writer's thoughts and feelings.

About Brass

Brass is an yellow alloy of copper and zinc in varying proportions with quantities of lead tin and iron brass is very malleable, fusible ductile and readily cast and machined, Muntz or yellow metal is a variety of brass containing 60% copper, As it resists corrosion well, it is largely used for ship propellors, bows and fittings, corrosion means rusting away.

Some examples of what brass can make:

1. electrical fixtures
2. unexpensive jewelry
3. metal decorations
4. table lighter
5. trombone
6. screws
7. marine hardware

In the famous Praha football stadium, nearly everything in side the walls are made out of copper including the goalpost, the team that play here are Sparta Prague. Mallable means easy to work with, and very dicible.

The Poetic Function

In poetic writing it is taken for granted that "true or false?" is not a relevant question at the literal level. What is presented may or may not in fact be a representation of actual reality, but the writer takes it for granted that his reader will *experience* what is presented rather in the way he experiences his own memories, and not *use* it like a guidebook or map in his dealings with the world; that is, the language is not being used instrumentally as a means of achieving something, but as an end in itself. When Huck Finn said all Tom Sawyer's great stories were lies he was mistaking the function of the stories (the poetic function) and applying the "rules" of the other "game"—the transactional. So a reader *does* different things with the transactional and poetic writings: he uses transactional writing, or any bit of it, for any purpose, but who can say what we "do" with a story or a poem that we read, or a play we watch? Perhaps we just share it with the writer; and not having to *do* anything with it leaves us free to attend to its formal features (which are not explicit): the pattern of events in a narrative, the pattern of sounds and of images and, above all, the pattern of feelings evoked. In attending in this non-instrumental way, we experience feelings and values. The term *poetic* is used here in a narrower and more specific sense than in its general usage. We use it here in the sense of the Greek from which it was derived, to mean "created." Its examples in school use are the stories, poems, and plays which children write and read.

In the context of these function categories, it is perhaps worth drawing attention to the ways in which knowledge—and, by implication, learning—in secondary and higher education is organized: systematically by subject disciplines and presented in the explicit, often specialized and generally formal language of those who know to those who are beginning to

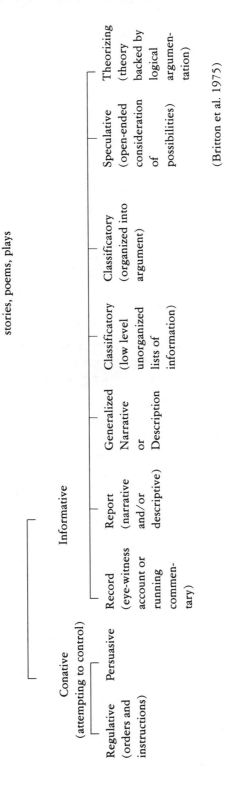

TRANSACTIONAL ←--- ←--- EXPRESSIVE ---→ ---→POETIC

stories, poems, plays

Conative (attempting to control)

Informative

Regulative (orders and instructions)

Persuasive

Record (eye-witness account or running commentary)

Report (narrative and/or descriptive)

Generalized Narrative or Description

Classificatory (low level unorganized lists of information)

Classificatory (organized into argument)

Speculative (open-ended consideration of possibilities)

Theorizing (theory backed by logical argumentation)

(Britton et al. 1975)

know. In contradistinction, the kind of knowledge (and way of learning) that goes on outside school is random, unsystematic, and may or may not be linked by the learner to school knowledge. The bridge between systematic and unsystematic knowledge would seem to be the learner's own language, his own formulations, which are the means by which he incorporates the new into his existing corpus of knowledge. Most people do this by talk, but in school the expressive and poetic functions of writing give children opportunities to recognize and evaluate new knowledge and new experiences and thereby gain self-knowledge.

Our transactional category clearly needed to be broken down in terms of the kind of transaction undertaken, since the great majority of school writing is of this kind. If teachers want to gain some idea of the range of writing opportunities that their pupils are getting—or not getting—*across the curriculum,* the diagram we used is one way of enabling them to find out.

A Sense of Audience: The Child and His Reader.

The Sense of Audience model arose from our reading of hundreds of writings with the aim of identifying who the writers saw as their audiences. The following are the categories we arrived at to help us in our descriptions of school writings.

Categories of a sense of audience
   1. Child, or adolescent, to self.
   2. Child, or adolescent, to trusted adult (teacher or others).
   3. Student to teacher—senior partner in a dialogue.
   4. Student to teacher—who shares a special interest with the student.
   5. Student to teacher—as Examiner.
   6. Student to other students or peer groups (known or unknown).
   7. Writers to their readers—public audiences.

The notion of audience has powerful implications for school writing in spite of the fact that almost all of it is produced for one sort of reader, the teacher. What makes for differences between the pieces of writing is not, objectively, who the reader is, but how the writer *sees* his reader; and children see their teachers in very different ways. Not only may different children's views of the same teacher vary, but a child may see his teacher as a different sort of reader on different occasions. Furthermore, the process of writing is more complicated even than this suggests. The monitoring self is always a part of a writer's sense of audience, as well as those others—the class, friends, examiners sometimes, parents perhaps, and a shadowy "public"—who lurk behind his shoulder. In speech, the actual or potential feedback from the listener continuously modifies what is said because the audience is physically present—right there in front of you—and sooner or later will speak and thereby modify what you say next. In writing, there is no such feedback. The actual audience normally slips away into the background, leaving the writer free to pursue the meanings he wants to get down on paper. But somewhere, out of the direct focus of attention, a sense of an audience remains, ready to take shape when summoned, or stepping forward uncalled. We think it likely that one reason for the great amount of inert, inept writing produced by school students is that the natural process of internalizing the sense of audience, learned through speech, has been perverted by the use of writing as a testing or reproductive procedure at the expense of all other kinds of writing. When a writer's focus is on returning as exactly as possible what he has been given, the sense of any other audience, including the monitoring, reflective, independent self, disappears, leaving incomprehension, resentment or despair, or alternatively the satisfaction of producing something to satisfy someone else's demands. We think the following conversation throws light on some of these matters.

Andrew (a third-year boy) is talking to one of the project officers who knows his school and his teachers well. They are talking about Andrew's humanities project on "The Industries and Populations of Towns" and are referring to an anecdote he had included about slavery:

BN: There's an anecdote about a grave ... it was something about slaves—it was something about, er, in a cemetery near Harlow there's a gravestone which says on it "Here lies so-and-so, the property of somebody-or-other." How did you find that out?

A: Well, we just moved—'cos we don't live far from that end, we'll go to church fairly often, and we went round to see that church 'cos we saw it from the road and I like looking at gravestones and that and I saw it sort of fitted in with that.

BN: And who are you asking the question of "Rather unusual to put on a grave, don't you think?"

A: Well, that's to anyone who reads it.

BN: Do you think of your reader?

A: Yes.

BN: Who do you think of?

A: Anyone who reads it. Mainly Sir [his teacher is commonly called "Sir."] 'cos he reads it. And anyone else.

BN: But I mean, when you put a thing like that, or your jokes, do you think to yourself "How will Mr. S ... react?" or do you think in more general terms, how will anybody react—you know?

A: More general, I think, how would anyone.

BN: You do? So you're not just thinking of him.

A: Oh, no.

BN: Would you, I mean, it's kind of a bit odd because you say that mostly these just get stockpiled, you know, so they're not read by anyone else normally.

  A: Not really, no. But we're always told to write it as though we're trying to explain to someone else of our own age—so we just get used to it.

BN: So you do it, I mean you do actually think of other people reading it even though you don't expect them ever to do it?

  A: Yes, that's how we have to. They always write out "as if to someone of your same age," and you've got to tell them about it.

It seems that Andrew, in his writing, takes account both of his actual audience—his teacher—and some potential wider audience. Earlier in this conversation he had said that he often puts jokes in his writing because his teacher enjoys them and he himself likes them. This seems near to a trusted adult audience, which we think the most fruitful in developing writing ability because it allows a writer to experiment with safety. Andrew also understands the convention which requires him to write *as if for* some particular audience—"they always write out 'as if to someone of your own age,' and you've got to tell them about it"; and he understands that this convention allows him to express his own opinions and feelings within the framework of the "as if" situation.

We have found an increasing number of teachers who have tried to create situations involving an audience other than themselves, real or imagined, as a context for the writing they have asked their pupils to do. On the whole this tends to come from teachers concerned with the humanities. In the sciences and among older students, there is perhaps an unspoken sense that this is a device for younger children or for less serious studies, yet the American psychologist George Kelly in a paper called "The Language of Hypothesis" describes an attitude and a corresponding use of language which would help to bridge the gap between the known and the unknown—which, of course, is just what teachers are trying to do when they ask children to write "as if they were . . ." or "what would happen if . . ."; Kelly calls this the use of the invitational mood. He says that at moments of risk we would be greatly helped if we deliberately abandoned the indicative mood and operated in the invitational mood with its language form, "let us suppose. . . ." He says that this procedure suggests that things are open to a wide range of constructions and that "there is something in stating a new outlook in the form of a hypothesis that leaves the person himself intact and whole." When students reflect on their work or even report what they know, they put themselves at risk in terms of their teacher audience, or any audience for that matter, and we would stress the value of the invitational mood with regard both to a hypothetical audience and to hypothetical ideas. We quote an example here because the "as if" situation is directly one of audience: "Suppose that you wanted to explain what diffusion is to a younger child who has not done any science and does not know what molecules are":

Explaining diffusion

We all know that gases are invisible, in other words we can't see it there but it is present. Gases are made up of molecules, for the moment let us call molecules "marbles." These marbles are present in solids as well, but here they are squeezed together and are unable to move. But in a gas the marbles (which cannot be seen with the human eye, only with an electronic microscope) move about freely and do not move in one specific direction, they move at random. . . .

This, of course, was an "exercise," but it was also a game played by the children and the teacher—a combined knowledge and language game. The pupils had to manipulate their knowledge and their language to serve an audience other than themselves and their teacher; and, as their teacher observed, "you only really understand ideas like these when you can play with them," i.e. suppose this, and suppose that, in Kelly's terms.

The two models of "Function" and "A Sense of Audience" make it possible for us to look at the range of writing which children are doing in all their school work; and it allows us to be quite precise about the development of their ability to write appropriately for different purposes and different audiences, which was how we defined progress.

"Development is to a large extent a process of specialization and differentiation: we start by writing the way we talk to each other—expressively, and envisaging as our reader a single, real, known person; gradually we may acquire, *in addition,* the capacity to use the transactional and the poetic, and to write for an unspecified, generalized or unknown audience. Further, this differentiation ideally occurs as a result of coming to hold those adult purposes for which the mature forms of writing have been evolved, and of learning to anticipate the needs of different and remoter audiences. So the development of writing abilities is partly conditional on the more general development of the child out of egocentrism; but that general development may itself be aided by the practice of writing" (Martin et al., 1973).

Yet, the findings of our survey showed that the range of kinds of writing that children have opportunities to use in the secondary school narrowed drastically as they moved from year one to year seven. The dominant kind of writing was classificatory for an examiner audience. James Britton (Britton et al., 1975), commenting in the Research Report says, "If, as we had predicted, the development of writing abilities showed itself as a growing range of kinds of writing shaped by thinking processes, we should have expected to find in the sample a great deal of expressive writing in the early years, in all subjects (instead of the 6% we actually found) and an increase in the later years of classificatory, speculative, and theoretical writing, as well as persuasive and poetic—all these compensating for a reduction in the expressive; and at the same time, a proportion of expressive writing maintained and developing into its maturer forms and purposes.

"It would appear, however, that the pressures to write at a classificatory level of the informative—and in the main for an audience of the teacher as examiner—were great enough to inhibit early expressive writing and to prevent all but minimal development into the more abstract levels of the informative; strong enough at the same time to cut down drastically in the seventh year the output of the poetic. We believe an explanation for this unexpected narrowing of the range must be sought *in the whole curriculum and its objectives* [author's italics]. The small amount of speculative writing suggests that, for whatever reason, curriculum aims did not include the fostering of writing that reflects independent thinking; rather, attention was directed towards classificatory writing which reflects information in the form in which both teacher and textbook traditionally present it."

References

James Britton, Anthony Burgess, Nancy Martin, Alex McLeod and Harold Rosen. *The Development of Writing Abilities 11–18.* Macmillan, 1975.

Nancy Martin, Peter Medway, Pat D'Arcy and Harold Smith. *Why Write?* Schools Council/London University Institute of Education Joint Project: Writing Across the Curriculum, 1973.

Edward Sapir. *Culture, Language and Personality.* Berkeley and Los Angeles, University of California Press, 1961.

7

What Are They Up To?

Some Functions of Writing

A study of a week's output in writing from three classes,
one aged 7, one aged 11, and one aged 9

This study of all that the children wrote in a sample week is intended to document from actual examples some of the relationships between language and experience which James Britton has explored elsewhere. In doing this I have attempted to apply some of the ways of looking at children's writing that we used in the enquiry into the development of writing abilities at the secondary level carried out at the London Institute of Education under the sponsorship of the Schools Council.

I am going to look in some detail at what seem to be the functions of the different kinds of writing done by three classes in three different schools; one aged six to seven years, one aged nine to ten, and one aged ten to eleven. All the written work that each child did in one week was collected and read many times in an attempt to answer the question: "What are these children using this language for?"

I have tried to answer this question in terms of the broad distinctions of language use that James Britton describes, so that when the terms "expressive," "referential," and "poetic" are used, they will have the same meaning as he attaches to them.

I begin the story with the seven-year-olds at the stage when the children have internalized a good deal of the talk they have been sharing in for about five years, and are now able to engage in the dialogue in the head of which writing is a modified expression; that is, they "speak" on paper at

Published in *Children Using Language*, A. Jones and A. Mulford (eds.), © Oxford University Press, 1971.

some length, without the physical stimulus of another person who keeps the talk going. It is true, of course, that they are writing for their teacher who will read what they have written and will "reply" to it in some way, but she is not "listening"—and participating—as they write. In their writings (as in their spoken utterances) they are discovering themselves, and discovering the world around them.

A. The Seven-year-olds: A Week's Work

The school

The work came from a class of 24 children (unstreamed), 11 boys and 13 girls, mostly aged 7 (or nearly 7) in a County Infant School in a commuter area for Wolverhampton.

This written work represents only a proportion of all the things the children engaged in during the week under review; but it does represent *all the writing* they did.

The school has an informal organization with a varying pattern of self-chosen and teacher-directed work. Each day begins with news-writing (or telling) as they come in to school and settle down; parents can also come for this first half hour of the day, which is social, informal and rooted in talk.

This is followed by assembly with some music—again this is informal—the children sit on the floor in self-chosen groups and news is exchanged.

After this the children and their teachers pursue various activities as they wish; but the children's writings show that certain features in the week's work are constant. Though no two writing books are alike, some things have been done by all. Each child, for instance, has done some mathematics; each child has done some science: all begin the day with a diary entry; all have written at least one story ("My Story"). Besides these items, there are letters to their Headmistress, newspaper reports written by them, poems and a few informative pieces about objects, creatures or operations that have interested the writers, and very occasionally something informational such as an account of the Romans in Britain.

So the overall picture shows two areas of teacher-directed work that all write up in a similar way—mathematics and science—and outside these, any area of their experience may be written about. Some children who will have been spending more time on other activities do less writing than others, but the direction (with time allotted) towards diaries on the one hand and stories on the other means that every child uses his own language to make something of his outer and inner experiences for himself.

The children belong to the County Library and they may change their books every dinner hour. Furthermore, there are books set about the school where they catch the eye. So the writing that appears in the children's books must be seen against a background of other people's writing (books) and much talk with each other and with adults (the children constantly go into the Headmistress's room, which is also the staff room, to talk to her, ask questions or look for their friends).

The writings

The average amount written by each member of the class was 20 full pages, excluding pictures, and this covered about 15 different items; 10 of the stories are between 4 and 10 pages in length. The writings reflect the children's lives at home and in school, their special interests (animals, football, birthdays, play, friendships, food, etc.), their fantasies, their relationships with teachers, families and friends, and also the work they had been doing in school.

Within the average of 15 different pieces of written work each child had made four or five diary entries and had written one or two generally long stories; he had also done two or more pieces of work headed "Mathematics" and two or three brief reports of scientific experiments. Over and above this minimum most children had written a good many other things. The only direct copying from books that occurred in this sample was a brief item of "National news" which about half the children added at the end of their diary entries; often this was copied verbatim but not always.

The referential and the poetic

The first thing one observed about the writing which all children did was that the language of the personal news and stories was sharply different from the language of the mathematics and science. James Britton suggests that children's early writing will rely heavily on their experience of speech and is likely to be of a kind that we should classify as expressive, and that, as they gain experience, we should expect to find it being modified in two directions, sometimes towards the referential and sometimes towards the poetic.

In these writings we found such differentiation; the personal news items are very like written-down speech, and though often not overtly expressive, if by an act of imagination one re-sets these bald statements into their context of seven-year-old voices, gestures, hesitations and facial expressions, one can be in no doubt that these are personal declarations—as are all the items which are initiated by the children; the stories, however, in addition to being highly expressive have formal elements which mark them out as different from the news items. The science and mathematics are different in another way; they have been directed towards the referential and are not primarily expressive, though as we shall see, some of them contain expressive elements, and I am later going to suggest that the function of

these expressive elements is to relate these outer discoveries to the writers'
inner world-picture.

The diaries

"In written speech," says Vygotsky, "we create the situation and represent it to ourselves." Here is what David wrote as his news item for May
5th:

> Today it's my birthday and I had a spiaragrath and a airfix Bumper
> Books and I played with my spiarograht and when Daddy brought me
> to school hes going back and his going to play with my spiarograth
> and today Gary is coming to tea and we will play subuiteo and foot-
> ball and with my spiarograth and we might have a game at table soc-
> cer and Gary will have to go at about 8 o'clock and I will go and help
> him carry his things then I will go home and go to bed.

He has re-created some of the events of the day by recalling them and
framing them in words; furthermore he has created the shape of some future events as he expects they will happen. This diary item, and hundreds
like it, is closely tied to the here and now of actual events; it is a representation based on memory and experience and its order is the order in which
events happen to us, one after the other; the bald statements in temporal
order demand few other connectives than "and" and "then," and its only
coherence lies in the fact that all the statements are so joined. It is essentially written-down speech. David speaks on paper just as he would if he were
giving an oral account of what he did yesterday, but under this apparent
similarity lurks a tremendous intellectual and linguistic difference. It is an
imagined and not a real conversation that is taking place; there is no actual
listener as he writes, and his sense of an audience, or someone to communicate with, is secondary to the fact that he is above all making a representation of his experience to himself.

In speech the changing motives of the speakers determine at every
moment the turns that it will take. It does not have to be consciously directed—the dynamic situation takes care of that. Writing, on the other hand, is
detached from the actual situation and requires deliberate analytical action.
The young writer at 7 years old has to be aware of the sound structure of
each word and reproduce it in alphabetical symbols, and he has to be explicit in a way that he never has to be in speech. Above all he is without the
stimulus of the actual situation and the speech of other people. Vygotsky
observes that the motives for writing are often far from the child—are
more intellectualized and further removed from actual needs. And think of
the laboriousness of it! It is not, therefore, surprising that at seven, relatively little of their experience is verbalized in writing—David's diary items
about his birthday, for example, carry little sense of how he felt about it; his

feelings are not events and the familiar narrative form does not demand it. In speech his feelings would be expressed in tone of voice and movement and tempo and volume. The direct expression of self-awareness comes later; at seven, judging from the diaries, patterns of events would seem to be as much as the children can manage, though the stories suggest that here self-awareness is beginning to creep in.

Occasionally a more extended item appears—an anecdote for instance, and any such extension demands a correspondingly more complex language. Here is what Mary wrote:

> On Saturday morning I went down to the shops with mummy to get some stuff for the party when I was there I saw Mrs. Bowaller I took her to see Shandy who was in the car I told her that he was a hunting dog mr. Bowaller wanted to know what things he hunted and I said that he hunted anything and mr. Bowaller said I hope he dosnt hunt teachers I am off. But Andrew said that he didnt.

The greater explicitness of her re-creation of the shopping incident makes demands on her language of a different sort from David's bald items; e.g. "... I went down to the shops ... *when I was there* I saw Mrs. Bowaller I took her to see Shandy *who was in the car.*" Then she moves into reported speech and out of it into direct speech and ends with the statement "But Andrew said that he didnt."

The stories: moving towards the poetic

Here is another kind of representation: this one is not tied to the actual—to the way things *are*—but is a representation of the way the writer *feels* about things. Ian wrote:

> One day there lived a farmer he was very very rich and this farmer had a son and when the farmer died he gave the farm to his son and also gave his money to his son and his son felt very proud because he had the horses and the cows and the pigs and the cattle and sheep but the farmers son was not satisfied because he wanted some hens and a hen house built for him and one day he heard of some men coming round building things for people and he said to himself I'll ask thees men to build me a hen house and buy some hens and be happy. and perhaps there wouldn't be any need to have anything else on the farm because the farm might be full of animals but if not he might buy some more sheep to put in the cattle shed some more pigs to put in the pig sty but if there is too much on the farm he would sell some and might be even richer then he would have much more money than he had last time and at this he was so happy that he danced all round the farm untill he was very very tired out and so he lay down and went to sleep and he dremt a dreem that he had never dremt befor

and it was a very nice dream and he dremt that a fairy cam in the night and when he saw the fairy he couldn't beleave what he saw because by the fairy was a hen house and when he went by the hen house a flash of light came and the next thing he saw was some hens flying about and half of them coming out of the hen house to start flying. and some of them came with their mothers so there mothers could teach them to fly like other hens. and at there the farmers son whoke up and to his surprise there was a hen house right by him and the next thing he did was to look at his money to see if he had got enough to buy some hens. and when he looked he had just enough and so he went strate away and bought some hens to put in the hen house.

and when he had bought the hens he thought of something els and he thought of building a well and so he bought some bricks with his money and started to buld a well with them and it took him a very long time to buld the well and he got very tired so he had a rest and something to eat and drink and then went out and started to get on with the well and while he was bulding the well he thought about his farther and how he died untill he had nearly finished and then he had his tea and finished the well. then he said he will get some water and fill the well up with it and got a proper well.

Here is something very different going on. So different that it is important to make it clear that this story is very like all the other stories in certain ways, though no two children wrote about the same characters or events, and the features which make this story so different from the diaries are shared to a lesser or greater extent by all the stories.

In the first place it is very long, though it is by no means the longest. All the children's stories are longer than anything else they write.

In the second place, the sense that a story is something long and full makes entirely different demands on their language resources, and brings within reach language forms to fit the needs of an extended narrative; and they know this because they are familiar with stories. This writing is not just written-down speech.

Ian's story, for instance, is not about things as they are but as they might be; it is about thoughts and feelings and reasons and speculations. He wrote:

> ... one day he (the farmer's son) heard of some men coming round building things for people and *he said to himself* I'll ask these men to build me a hen house and *be happy, and perhaps there wouldnt be* any need to have anything else on the farm *because* the farm *might be* full of animals, *but if not he might* buy more sheep to put in the cattle shed ... *but if* there is too much on the farm *then he would* sell some and *might be even richer*. ...

Here he is dealing with *possibilities,* and possibilities can only exist in the mind. His story is only partially structured by the chronological order of events as they happened. In order to cope *explicitly* with possibilities he has to use "the complex internal organization that language itself provides for representing relations of sequence and hierarchy and consequences." This is a long way from the simple narrative pattern in the diaries of things as they happened.

Furthermore, to show that this greater richness and complexity is a function of story-writing and not an individual difference here is Ian's diary entry for May 5th:

> On Saturday we went to watch my daddy play criket ... and while we were watching Me and My brother went to watch the bowling and while we were watching the bowling a boy came up to us and we made friends with him and his name was neal and I got my ball and played football and my brother was in goal and after one of us had got ten goals we played criket with the boys bat and ball and then we had diner and then we played football for a bit and then it started to rain and so we went home.

This differs little from the other diary entries; its pattern of events is chiefly strung together by "and" and "then," and it makes no attempt to verbalize his feelings.

In the third place, stories deal with another aspect of possibility at an altogether different level. The characters and events make a *symbolic* representation of how things might be ... "Once upon a time there was a guinea pig ...," "One day there lived a farmers son. ..." When they are freed from the constraints of the actual, as they are in story-writing, the children explore all sorts of possible patterns that events might take. Their stories are shaped to their desires and fears, and like dramatic play allow them to verbalize symbolically areas of experience which are impossible for them to express in explicit form. One boy, for instance, wrote two stories and a further whole book about two children (or two animals) who went walking and could not find their way home. As the children's preoccupations change, so the themes of their stories change. Preoccupations are, of course, states of feeling and these determine the events of the story, but in addition the children feel it appropriate and necessary to make explicit reference to how their characters felt. Ian says:

> the farmers son *felt very proud.* ... but he was *not satisfied* because he wanted some hens ... I'll ask thees men to buld me a hen house and buy some hens and *be happy.* ... at this he was *so happy that he danced all round the farm* ... it was a *very nice dream.*

In the fourth place, the stories show the children's language moving from the expressive towards the poetic. They are much more shaped than written-down speech, in that they show formal elements. These seven-year-olds are quite clear that they are writing stories, and that stories are recognizable and exist "out there." Sometimes they head their writing—"My Story"; often they make a more ambitious superscription such as,

> The Car that Talked
> Written by Mark Tolley
> Pictures by Mark Tolley
> Published by Mrs. Thompson.

Their past experience of literature is in the background all the time; they were familiar with stories before they could write—I am not, of course, suggesting conscious imitation, only that they have a notion of what stories are like from their past experience of listening to stories, and equally they know that they are now engaged in writing a story.

They begin in the way they expect stories to begin: "One day there lived a boy . . ."; "Once upon a time there lived a little girl . . ."; "Once upon a time it happened that . . ."; "Once there lived a rabbit . . ."; "Once upon a time there was a man and he was a carpenter. . . ." The formula "One day there lived . . ." may seem a little odd; probably we should regard it as a broad verbal gesture indicating that a story is about to begin—the formula *sounds* like the beginning of a story and has no exact meaning.

The other formal element which characterizes the stories is the repetition of situation. Consider Ian's story quoted above; first his account of what he wanted, then his dream in which he got it, then his transformation of the dream into reality—all dealing with hens and a hen house. David's story shows this patterning element even more clearly:

> One day there lived a boy his name was peter and he liked pets and he had a fish, a dog, a cat, a rabbit and one day he went to bed and in the morning his fish was dead so he went to bed the next morning he found out that his Dog was dead *he was very sad* so he went to bed and the next morning he found that his cat was dead so he went to bed and he found that his rabbit was dead and he had to save his pocket money and he got a cat first and then he got a fish and then got a dog and then got a rabbit last of all and he was not sad he was glad that he had pocket money and he only just had enough pocket money to buy all he wanted.

It looks as if the formal beginnings and the repetitions of events are features that make a story recognizable—"this is how it goes." Few of them are concerned to end their stories unless "they all lived happily ever after" fits what they want to say, and a good few of them lose their grasp of their individual "construct"—the pattern of events that they *wanted* to make—and slip back into the pattern of what happened yesterday. What they write then looks very like an extended diary item. Nicola, for instance, writes a very long story that begins:

> Once upon a time there was a guinea pig and he lived in a shop with lots of other guinea pigs . . . and a little girl and her mummy came in . . . (they buy the guinea pig and take it home) . . . and Jane played with her toys and her Mummy did some washing up and then Janes Mummy made the tea and then Mummy brought the dinner in and when they had finished Mummy washed up the dishes and then she put them away. . . .

This goes on for eight more pages and the guinea pig is mentioned only once (four pages later) when she goes to feed him before she goes to school. Her language is still tied to the memory of actual experience; she cannot dissociate it enough from *actual* past situations to improvise about *possible* situations as can the other children whose work has been quoted.

In contrast with this, here is Mary's story (one of her diary items is cited earlier). She is completely in control of what she wants to say and is able to take a familiar story as her starting point and improvise upon it to produce her own version:

> Once upon a time it happened that a little Foal was boran at a farm. It was a black foal the only white was a star on his forehead. He was a *very happy* Foal at the farm untill his mother died of a very bad disease. Everybody *was sad* because she was a very good horse. A few years later when he was a grown horse he was sold to a girl who *thought he was mavles* She teached him how to trot canter and Jump and all the things a good horse should know then they tried to think of a name. At last one of the family said I think Black Beauty would be a good name dont you. yes said the girl whose name was Alice yes I do So his name was Black Beauty.

This story is a long way from speech—"it happened that . . ."; "when he was a grown horse . . ."; "she teached him how to *trot canter and Jump* and all the things a good horse should know . . ."; "At last one of the family said. . . ." Moreover, she is beginning to use punctuation. Her sense that she is making a construct in the written language is more fully realized than many of the others'. Right at the other extreme is what Andrew wrote in his diary entry for May 5th:

> Monday May 5th I am going to play at digers and I will have my tip loding car and I am going to have my big pece of rok will go have my big lorys out and I will dig and I will have my soligs (soldiers) as werk men and I will dig deeper and deeper in the ground and I will triy and make a big hole and the solidigs will then make a hut for then to live in and I will make a tunal in the tunal will be a shelten from a

avalanche and ther will be Balke mis for the men to look in the pit and ther will be a big lory will be a garag and the soligs will have to make a big gun will go to the owory and dow all the things that ned blowing up.

This seems to be a written version of the kind of running commentary that young children often speak aloud as *they play with their toys;* but because it is written, not spoken, and because the boys are not actually there, Andrew writes his story in the future. Most of the children's diaries are concerned with real events. To Andrew this imagined situation is more important and operates more powerfully than the actual events of his life. This is the sole news item for May 5th. His entry for the next day is very similar. Adult criteria of written language are inappropriate in writing such as this. The power and tenacity of imaginative play are something to be remembered in planning activities which foster children's learning.

Mathematics and science: moving towards the referential

The language of mathematical and scientific items in the children's books is not self-initiated; a general pattern has been formulated by the teacher and is clearly intended to provide the basic form which will report each child's specific findings, i.e. to accommodate *individual* discoveries and *common* conclusions. Under the heading "Mathematics" Timothy wrote:

My pencil measures 7 inches
My book measures 8 inches downways, 13 inches
      half cross ways
My longest finger measures 3 inches
My shortest finger measures 2 inches
My thumb measures 2 inches
I am 39 inches round my head.

All the children who wrote about measuring had measured whatever they liked, but all had set down their findings in this way.

Again, 10 of the children had chosen to work on a graph (histogram) to show preferences of various kinds. The work of all is headed "Graph to show favourite...." (pets, flowers, pop groups, etc.). They have been shown how to set out the graph and record people's preferences, and how to state the results. Here are David's results:

14 people like Everton
 3 people like Liverpool
10 people like Wolves
 4 people like West Brom

The favourites are Everton
They are fantastic

And Mary wrote:

From my graph I can tell that there are 13 people who like dogs. ther are 3 people who like cats. ther are 3 people who like rabbits. ther is 1 person who likes guinea pigs, there are 0 people who like hamsters.

I think it is a sheme for hamsters Because they are suche nice creahs

Clearly, in this work the mode of setting out, and the pre-ordained impersonal language for recording their findings, is part of the ideas that the teacher is leading them into. She had provided them (loosely) with the referential language model of the adult world, but these seven-year-olds make their impersonal recordings of the preferences of their classmates and sometimes add comments that are purely expressive. In these transitional writings one has, as it were, caught the language on its way from being very like speech to becoming very like a particular form of adult writing which is almost purely referential. One has also caught a glimpse of the way in which information is assimilated; it is immediately brought to the bar of individual evaluation; past experience and present feelings sweep in to help incorporate this chunk of objective information into existing views of how things are:—Everton "are fantastic"; "... [hamsters] are suche nice creahs." Later such evaluations will be edited out as irrelevant, but at this stage I suggest they are performing a fundamental role in learning by enabling the young writer to relate his new knowledge to himself.

Impersonal writing

The other set of writings that all the children did were reports of experiments with air. The first one is headed "All about Air"—a promising title—but the experiments seem to have taken on something of the character of a conjuring performance. Yvonne wrote:

All about air
Air is invisible
Air takes up space
we put a handkerchief
in a Jar and it did
not get wet because
it had Air in the Jar

She continues:

Warm air rises
[diagram]
we put lit paper in a

Jar and we put a
piece of cardboard
under neath the Jar
and we put another
Jar under neath the
other side and the
somke rises

All the reports of the experiments are similar to this. None of them conveys the sense that the children have entered into and understood what they are doing—as their reports of measuring and of making graphs did; none of them contains the expressive elements which indicate that they are making this new learning their own.

Piaget's well-known experiment in which the young children thought that a tall thin jar held more water than a short fat jar even when he poured the liquid straight from one to another is startling evidence that children of this age cannot grasp this kind of reasoning. The very idea of a scientific experiment involves setting up the situation in such a way that only one explanation is possible; i.e. to rule out all alternative possibilities. It is precisely this mode of thinking that Piaget believes to be beyond the powers of young children. It seems likely that these meaningless reports reflect the mumbo-jumbo appearance of the experiments to the children. Children do learn what the world is like from observation—smoke rises from chimneys, bonfires, cigarettes and forbidden matches; they feel draughts and rushing wind and fly kites, but they neither require nor can cope with the kind of verification that controlled experiment is aimed at.

Furthermore, this particular work in science, concerned as it is with generalization (air takes up space; warm air rises) raises some very sharp issues that go beyond the Junior School. There are many important notions which we could never arrive at from our own experiences. These notions are presented to us by other people (teachers and books). Vygotsky calls these scientific or non-spontaneous concepts, and in order to make them our own—to grasp them—we have to make them grow downwards into our personal experiences which they can then unify and generalize; we turn the unfamiliar into the familiar by referring it to our representation of the world *as we have experienced* it. It would seem, therefore, that when a teacher is presenting children with generalizations, such as those quoted above, it is crucial to include interpretation in terms of their own familiar experiences as part of what is being learned. If children are encouraged to report their early scientific work in the impersonal and generalized mode adopted by adults and by conventions widely used throughout the secondary school, they are being prevented from using the most effective means by which these difficult and important areas of knowledge can be learnt. We shall see later how the ten-year-olds cope with science, but when experimental work is appropriate it should surely follow the lines of the Nuffield Junior scientific work which encourages the children to be explicit in all sorts of ways about their responses to observation, experiment and prediction. The more abstract and generalized the notions, the more important become the interpretations from personal experience: the children need the opportunity to refer their new learning to "their representations of the world as they have experienced it."

Other items

I now want to consider the things the children wrote which were in no way directed. Ian and Jill each had 23 different items in their books; others had 21, 19, 17 and so on down to 9. These covered expressive letters to Mrs. Thompson, observations of animals, birds or treasured objects, what they called "newspaper articles" but were in fact stories starting from something in a newspaper: there was an account of the Romans in Britain, and a report of how milk bottles are crated. There were some poems and occasionally there were brief items copied from newspapers. Clearly any firsthand or secondary experience that interested them might be matter for writing. Such freedom of choice results in different kinds of writing beginning to appear. Where specific topics are set, as is the general pattern in secondary schools, such choices are not available and there may be a consequent loss of flexibility of language and even loss of the capacity to write in tentative or exploratory ways.

Language learning is a matter of improvising upon models and gradually becoming aware that you are doing so. Speech takes its differing forms from actual situations; thus talk to strangers is different from talk with familiars, and talk with a friend of the same age is different from talk with a friendly adult; talk with a parent is different from talk with your Headmistress, even when it is Mrs. Thompson. When speech begins to be written down, it very early reflects the differences of situations, and the different language models that surround the children begin to affect how they write, just as speech situations affect their talk. I have referred to the children's clear sense that a story (or a poem) is something "out there," a construct that you make with words, and that this sense can only come from their familiarity with literature.

It is not so easy to trace other models but one can say that the children have a sense of available forms. One knows that the impersonal mode is rarely a part of their language experience at this age, yet it does occur in their writing. Two boys wrote identical pieces about crating milk—it followed some arithmetic about pints and quarts of milk. Nicholas and Mark wrote:

> When the milk *is taken* to the dairy on milk lorrys *it is got out* of the crates by a big graber and then *it is taken* to a big machinin that wash-

> es it and then they dry it and *it is time to fill* the bottles again and then *they have there tops on* then the graber puts them back in the crates.

This is the only instance of the passive voice in all the writing and it is perhaps significant to see how confusing it is to the writers. The use of "it" and the passive make them lose their sense of the grammatical subject. At first "it" refers to the milk but it rapidly becomes the bottles and when they write "it is time to fill the bottles again" this new "it" disrupts the structure and with some relief they revert to the active voice—"then the graber puts them back in the crate." This is not a kind of language they are familiar with yet. I suspect that this is untransmuted secondary experience; had it been firsthand experience I think it would have been described as they saw it and the language would have been much more sure.

When Ian writes about the Romans, even though he is dealing with secondary experience, he makes it entirely his own. He writes:

> Many years ago when the roamans lived they bult long strate roads and very good buildings because they were civilised people and very clever and strong and one day when the roamans knew a very lot about England they said to thereselfs we will go to that countery and so they made very strong boats and sailed across the sea but they had to have many fights before they came to England and when they came to England some people who were already there wernt very strong so some ran away to Wales and some ran away to Scotland but some stayed and joyend on to the romans army and the romans invayded ingland for two thousand years. . . .

It is interesting to compare this self-chosen account with pieces in other classes set by the teacher as a test. The orientation is different. Ian assumes that what interests him will interest his reader, so in writing about these past events he has shaped the facts to his own order and view of the world with a different purpose from that of the test situation.

In addition to the varying kinds of language that children encounter in the course of their lives at home and at school, there are the specific models that people teach them. I have quoted instances of these earlier in this article in commenting on the children's writing in mathematics and science; some of the poems written would also come in this category of taught models, since a generalized notion of a poem as something that rhymes at all cost is very widespread.

As one looks at the writings based on taught models one is struck by their relative lack of success compared with what the children learn for themselves by encountering all sorts of language experience and using what they feel to be appropriate as they go about their daily occupations.

B. The Eleven-year-olds: A Week's Work

The school

The work of this class came from 34 children, 16 boys and 18 girls, mostly aged eleven (or nearly eleven) in a County Primary School in a recently developed area of Staffordshire. This school, like the last one, has an informal way of operating; children and teachers talk to each other informally a great deal; the Headmaster, when he can, sits down to talk to the children as he goes round the school; there are new books set about the place, tanks of fish, exhibitions of poems, stories, pictures and things made.

In looking at the work of eleven-year-olds in this school we were asking the same question as before: "What are the children using their language for?" but we chose a school that was very much like the Infants school in its policy, i.e. informal talk, books—including a lot of literature—and a large measure of self-directed work were dominant features. In neither school were the classes streamed.

The writings

The teacher's notes for this class of 34 children show that the starting point for all the writings was a common one, i.e. none of the work was self-initiated, but given a common starting point, the children took off in all sorts of varied directions. The starting points in this week's work were:

1. Something felt, seen or heard during the holiday (May 1st);
2. The history of May Day celebrations;
3. Mathematics: children were asked to record measurements without using rulers, etc.: history of thumbs, cubits and yards: the need for standard measurements—decimal system;
4. Radio-vision (wireless commentary and filmstrip of the Great Barrier Reef) accounts written; work on a communal frieze:
5. Reports of what they had read this week;
6. Friday answers to general knowledge questions given on Monday;
7. Pond Dipping or Pond Discovery;
8. First chapter read of *Stories of King Arthur and His Knights:* children wrote dialogue or stories; scrap paper used for play-writing—it gave more expressiveness and informality;
9. Discussion on hunting: film on stag hunting talked about: extracts read from *Tarka the Otter:* fox hunting and beagling discussed (beagling from first hand experience): *To See the Rabbit* by Alan Brownjohn was read; the children then wrote in any way they liked.

In addition, the children chose any piece they liked from their English book and copied it (their own writing—some chose to copy poems they had written).

As one would expect with children in their last year in the Primary school, there is a great increase in the amount of secondary experience, but although there is a common starting point in topic, information, film, literature, etc., there is no expectation that there will be a common finishing point, that all will need to have learnt exactly the same things. In fact the reverse is true; the children clearly expect that they will proceed in their own directions in their own ways. There is no attempt to impose any particular form on how they write or display their work except that they mount it on white sheets of paper so there is a sense that it should look good and have drawings and pictures as well as writing—hence their teacher's remark about doing their plays on scrap paper when she wants the focus on getting the language down without attention to presentation. The teacher helps them as much as they want while they are writing but no corrections at all are made on the actual work.

The results of this freedom to write and explore as they wish are twofold: first they do not edit out the expressive features of their writing when dealing with the referential—pond life for instance, or the Great Barrier Reef—in an attempt to attain objectivity. Their writing includes their subjective response to their exploration of the world around. Articulating their response is a step towards self-awareness. Cassirer says, "If I put out the light of my own personal experience, I cannot see and I cannot judge the experience of others" (*Essay on Man*). This remains true of all new experience (or learning) at whatever age it is encountered.

Second, and this is really a consequence of the first, the children write in all sorts of ways. They are sensitive to the language that they meet in books and from their teachers and one can see the influence of the models they are meeting reflected in their work. Had they all been taught a particular way to write their science (or geography?—Great Barrier Reef) this exploration of different modes would not have happened. Both expressive elements and variety of modes are illustrated below.

Moving towards the referential: participant language

Mathematics. Neil's measurements are recorded as follows:
Length of desk = 14 half thums
Width of desk = 16 half thums
21 Neil thums = 1 Neil cubit
2 Neil cubits = 2' 8"
33" = a nose to tip of finger yard
1 Neil foot = 9"

And Ani wrote:
The width of my desk is = 16 thumbs
The length of my desk is = $16\frac{1}{2}$ thumbs

I used my thumb
28 Anita thumbs = a Anita cubit
2 Anita cubits = 26¾ inches . . .

—and from here to the need for standard measurements and the decimal system. "I used my thumb," Anita records, and it is plain to see that an Anita cubit takes more Anita thumbs than does a Neil cubit, Neil thumbs. Individual measurements and expressive elements in the records bring the notion of a standard measure into their personal experience.

The importance of primary experience as the basis of learning is an axiom in this school and the children's own formulations of things they have done, seen and felt is regarded as an aspect of primary experience. I want now to look at three other pieces of work that the children did in this sample week which were all concerned with new information derived from secondary experience; I want to look at the way it was related to their first-hand experience and then to look at the various ways they dealt with it.

First, then, the way it was presented to the children:

1. Junior science (variously headed—Pond Dipping; Pond Discovery, etc.) (See item 7 above.) This work was based on a pond-dipping expedition; the children were told how to approach a pond, how to net the creatures, how they caught and ate their prey, how a fish breathes, etc. This provided a rich body of information rooted in firsthand experience; no one was in any doubt, for instance, about what a water scorpion looked like (observation) or how it ate its prey (information).

2. The Great Barrier Reef of Australia. Work on this was based on a film with commentary, together with discussion and re-showings of parts of the film to reinforce questions and discussion. The children wrote about it and made a frieze. Thus, though not firsthand experience, they saw what corals looked like and observed in the film the fish and other creatures that inhabited the reef. Many of them reported that they "made corals" to go on the communal frieze. This work again gave a rich body of new information which the visuals brought very near to firsthand experience.

3. The history of May Day celebrations. This was dependent on the teacher's words; it was history and remote from their own experience so it had to be recreated in each child's mind by the interpretation he was able to put on the teacher's words. They were then invited to write either a report or to write about May Day as if they had been present at the celebrations in some particular place. Where they chose to write as if they had been present ("My name is Arthur. I am going to tell you about May Day. . . .") they made it clear that they had understood this was a holiday in some sense like the special days they know themselves—Easter Monday for instance; where they wrote about it as history it tended to be a random collection of facts ("On the first day of May there was always rejoicings in the villages from as far back as the twelfth century. There were rejoicings on

May Day in the Bible. The villagers lived in cold huts all the winter," etc.).

Those who wrote about May Day as if they had been present at the events they had been told about were able to give their account the coherence of a story and they were able to interpret the facts in terms of people's behavior which was, of course, what the teacher was chiefly hoping for. But there is another point at issue. Not all kinds of information lend themselves to this treatment, and this raises sharply the problems of dealing with informational matter in writing. Here is this body of new information together with those parts of one's experience which relate to it. How does one set about engaging with it? Theoretically one can take any bit of it and start there—and this is what these children do; but once started, where does one go? Adults solve this problem in general, in terms of purpose and audience (as I am attempting to do in this article), and in particular by means of generalizations which provide the "skeleton" of the writing.

The situation, however, is different for children. They do not usually see themselves as explaining things to adults; they do not argue much in writing; they do not usually ask questions and try to answer them in writing, and they don't give instructions in writing. Their role is usually to receive instructions. So how are they to set about structuring informational material that they are asked to write about? Where do they begin, and where are they to go?

In the Secondary school one of the commonest purposes of writing is "to show that they know what the lesson was about"—a test situation in fact, with the teacher as the audience. Within this general direction the teacher usually structures what they are to write by giving a title or a question to be answered: "Industry and Farming in the South West of England" or "Becket's quarrel with Henry II." This, of course, is also often the procedure in Primary schools, but not always. In this class the children make their own titles to indicate what they are going to write about and they are free to describe and comment on whatever they like; any selection of facts and comments and any order that they may choose to impose are equally welcome—i.e. importance is placed upon the choice they make. This is not therefore a test situation; it is a situation of mutual trust and respect. But the children's freedom to move about as they wish within the subject matter does mean that their selection of items is eclectic, depending on what has caught their interest, and until they can begin to use generalizations, what they write inevitably has this random character. The writings of these eleven-year-olds where it is explicitly concerned with the world around them is very like the writing of the seven-year-olds in this respect, but one can begin to see the growing ability to use generalization and abstraction as a means of organization: "A pond can be very interesting, most people do not know what is among all the mud at the bottom" or "Limestone is coral's skeleton and its house." This is the development of conceptual thinking at work, and it is by this kind of thinking that they will learn to select and order referential material, but it is a late development, and we have plenty of evidence that generalizations imposed by the teacher are often meaningless to the children.

Let us now see how these children attempted to solve this problem of structuring their referential writing. Since this was an unstreamed class, there are big differences in the amounts and the quality of what was written.

The first thing one observes about the writing of this class is that it is all more or less expressive; there is no sense that any of the writing (except perhaps the mathematics) should be written in any given way, yet one can observe all sorts of background models influencing what they write. Only their accounts of their holidays are relatively uninfluenced by adult forms of writing; they are like speech or informal letters, and they differ from the personal writings of the seven-year-olds only in the enormous extension in the areas of experience that they verbalize. They are no longer little bald pieces but detailed representations of major and minor events in their lives. For example, Lyn wrote a piece that she called "A Few Days in the Garden"; here is part of it:

> . . . "Let's get the chairs out and play at houses" said Joycelin. We made two little houses. Soon it was dinner time. After dinner we went to a bunglo with Joycelins daddy. He mowed the lawns while we made daisy chains. We made a daisy chain that was as long as the bedroom and half as long again. Then we went to the bathroom. We both sat in the bath. Joycelin crept out and told me to go to sleep. She put the tap on and wet my clothes. Her daddy came in so we hid in the cupboard. . . .

In the other pieces (items 2 to 9 above) nearly all of them are trying out all sorts of other "voices" which they feel are appropriate according to the "stance" they have taken up in their inner dialogue. This is particularly clear in the writings that are moving towards the referential—"Pond Dipping," or the "Barrier Reef" or "May Day."

Here is what Lyn wrote; she bounces up like a puppy dog and says:

> Do you know what this is? A pond is the answer (colored picture). Fish (colored drawing). Water Spider (colored drawing). These are just two of the things that live in the pond. Of course there are more things. A fish breathes through its mouth and can only live in water. So if you get a fish out of water it will of course die. Like we would die if we were put in water for a long while and could not come out. A water spider lives in a bubble of air underneath the water (picture). A spider can also run across the water without getting its feet wet. (Colored drawing) This has a caddis fly inside.

This is very much as she would speak, and she tells only the items that interest her.

Sheila writes:

> It is all very interesting getting ready to go Pond Dipping with tins, jars and nets. When you get to the pond children shout, talk and frighten the fish away before they even start dipping. Afterwards when the talking has stopped, cast your nets in the water. About two minutes later lift your net out. Empty your catch in a tray, a white one is *best*. If you have a Pond Book with you, *it is a good idea* to look up some of your catch....

This is a very different "voice" from Lyn's; is it perhaps the teacher's tones that she has caught "... a white one is best...." and "... it is a good idea...."?

Here is another voice, Robert Farmer. This one begins with a rather surprising generalization, but he fails to *use* it to provide a framework for his piece—which has a consciously bookish and humorous tone:

> A pond can be anywhere, behind trees by the railway almost anywhere you think of there is likely to be a pond. When you have found a pond unknown to you and I the thousands of little creatures go into exile, they hide under stones under weeds and in the mud. One of the most interesting creatures in the pond is the water spider which spins a web under water and then graduly it takes down air and stores it in the new home it has built.
>
> Another interesting creature is the Caddis fly larvae this is an interesting creature because it is a tasty meal for any animal who feels a little peckish. But nature gave this creature sense to build a house of anything it can find wood, little stones, dead leaves, this provides protection against its enemys.

Then there is Martin's piece; he too feels it appropriate to begin with a generalization: "A pond is a small lake filled by vegertion." (I think "vegertion" means plants *and* animals to him). "Tadpoles, Sticklebacks and minowes are some of the most common ones."

Unlike most of the children he does not choose the most *interesting* creatures to describe but follows up his second generalization about the most *common* ones. He continues with a third generalization which he develops:

> Dragon flys are the enemy of most insects in the pond: when they are young they proul around like cats to catch insects.

He then goes on to describe the family life of sticklebacks. We can see in this account the beginning of the adult pattern of weaving in and out of the general and the particular. But this is no imposed pattern: "Dragon flys are the enemy of most insects in the pond: when they are young they proul around like cats . . ." Here is his own experience, his own language rooting his generalization in the particular.

Now let us look at what Neil Hackett writes; he heads his piece "Science." This I think is a pointer to how he thinks about it—yet another model, and a familiar one this time:

> In the pond there are many different kinds of creatures. Fish are a certain shape so that they can get through the water fast. They *are said* to be streamlined. *It is best when pond dipping* to put plant eating insects in one tank and meat eating insects in another. Caddis flies make their houses with anything they can get their feelers on. . . .

Although he has the scientific "voice" with its detached tone and impersonal phrases, his piece lacks any structuring in relation to the general statements that he begins by using, and his last item is pure speech. Up to that point he is imitating a model without *using* it.

And here is a very adult "voice"; Robert Lim writes:

> *A pond is full of life. A whole city in miniature may exist in a pond. The animals in the pond are either carniverous or vegetarian.* The carnivors are meat eaters and the vegetarians eat plants. *Of all the things* which live in the ponds the caddis fly larvae *is the one with the best camaflage.* It makes *a kind of shed out of the substance around it.* (drawing: caddis fly)
> The water spider has *an ingenious method* of breathing under water. He makes his den and then brings down air bubbles in his hind legs! (drawing: water spider)
> The fish breath by breathing in water and then *extracting its properties of oxygen by means of a type of grid.* (drawing)

His first paragraph shows generalizations being *used to structure* all the items in the paragraph. I think by "city in miniature" he is getting at the idea of an underwater community with its carnivors and vegetarians, and with carnivors around some of the creatures will need camouflage. Then he goes on to describe *methods* of breathing. His items are not random; to be concerned with *methods* of breathing under water implies a hierarchy of related ideas which is altogether different from Lyn's egocentrically interested report that water spiders can run across the water without getting their feet wet. Robert is deliberately and skilfully using a particular form of the written language, but he is not afraid to make his own improvisations when he needs to—"a kind of shed . . ." and ". . . and brings down air bubbles in his hind legs!" These improvisations reveal the crucial process of relating new phenomena to his existing knowledge.

Finally, somewhere between Lyn's and Robert's is Neal Jackson who wrote:

> What kind of world is a fish world? Imagine living in water all the time. There are many kinds of insects which crawl about the weeds and mud. Many are *unearthly like creatures.* Illustrated opposite is a caddis larvae made up of *bits and bobs* such as sticks and stones. Also there is the water scorpion which kills its enemies. First it kills them and then sucks out all the juices. Fish are streamlined for swimming. They breathe by swallowing water and extracting the oxygen from the water and pushing it out through his gills.

Neil hovers uncertainly between the personal and the impersonal; he cannot yet manage Robert's level but he is on the way to it and he improvises with similar felicity. His piece is essentially coherent because he structures it throughout towards his starting question—"What kind of world is a fish world?" and towards his answer to that question—"Many are unearthly like creatures."

In this loosely graded selection of writing one can see individual assimilation and shaping in the choice of items and the choice of "voice" to write in; but one can also see the beginnings of attempts to find a means of structuring—a general idea which will make sense of the scatter of particulars that follow. This groping for unifying concepts is a marked feature of the children's referential writing in this class.

I think two points arise from this set of writing. First, when children are free to select and order as they wish, they are also free to draw consciously—as Robert does—or unconsciously, on the language resources that are in their inner ears from their reading, from television viewing and from their teachers, and it is worth noting that in this set of work there were 34 different "voices." If they are taught a particular way of writing and are asked to recapitulate what they have been taught in a lesson, they cannot draw freely on these resources; neither can they attempt to shape what they write, and shaping in referential writing is *thinking* itself. In these 34 free pieces we can see all sorts of models being tried out. In other words, this same freedom allows them to use language creatively as a tool of understanding. At the points where they attempt to relate the new to their existing knowledge they improvise in terms of their own experience, and this is the only sure foundation for learning. ("Unearthly like creatures"; "a kind of shed"; "bits and bobs such as sticks and stones"; "limestone is coral's skeleton and its house.")

Second, and rather a different kind of point, because they are allowed to use language as an adult is free to do—without injunction—we are able to see the process of selecting and ordering at work.

The stories and poems: spectator language: moving towards the poetic

Both the stories and the poems are very different from those of the seven-year-olds. The obvious formal elements in both have disappeared. No one begins "Once upon a time," or "Once there lived . . ."; none of the stories has the repetitive patterning of events that is familiar in fairy tales and legends: but their basic purpose seems to be the same—the exploration of the possibilities of human behavior, possibilities that are shaped by the children's notions of how they would like things to be, or more rarely, how they fear things might be. The stories *seem* more realistic, less like fables or fairy tales, but although the peripheral details and settings and conversations may be realistic, the central pattern of events reveals that the children are still more concerned with how they feel about things than with how things are. Every child except one, for instance, makes his hunted creature either escape or die a quick death. (Item 9 in the list of work done in the sample week.) They are not concerned with the realities of the *events* of the hunt but with the different realities of the emotions of the hunter, or of the hunted or of their own preoccupations in disguise. So, instead of the obvious formal elements these stories are shaped by an interior coherence which arises from the stance that the writers adopt. Lyn writes:

> Hello my name is Tinker I am a little puppy dog. . . . I'm not really a huntsdog but I sneak out and join in. . . .

From then on her story is determined by what she sees and how she feels as a puppy dog sneaking out to join in the hunt. The seven-year-olds were not capable of this kind of interior coherence arising from the possibility of being someone else for a time.

Let us look for a moment at the complex tissue of possibilities that any narrative presents to a writer and try to see to what extent these children can take account of these. A writer is a spectator of imagined events and in spinning the web of his story he draws on his own experience and his experience of literature. First there is the pattern of events in all their fullness. Neal begins:

> The dogs split as they came through woods followed by about a dozen horsemen. They stumbled over a hillock squealing and barking.The dogs, mostly terriers and hounds jumped over a rickerty old stone wall except for the smaller dogs who tried to find a detour.

Here he is the narrator observing the scene from outside, as it were. A mature writer does not give equal weight and value to every item that he describes. He turns a kind of spotlight on some and represents them fully in words, as Neal has done in his opening. Other events are reported by a brief statement; Neil writes, "Everybody saw their quarry, a fox." Here the spotlight has been turned off but the thread of the narrative has been maintained and we are ready for the next bit of highlighting. In addition to the writer's bird's eye view of what is happening, he often interrupts his narrative to explain why something happened or why someone behaved as he did. Neal says, "The fox was taking a chance in trying to beat the dogs to the causeway"; and Robert says about his chief hound, ". . . getting overconfident he went over the stream." This is still the voice of the narrator but he has moved his focus from description of events to comment and explanation. But these areas are only part of all that is happening—which is the potential province of the writer. He may want to concern himself with how the hunters felt and their view of what was happening, or how the hunted creature felt. A mature writer may take any or all of these elements into his purview; what most of the children do is to take up a single clearly defined stance and structure what they write from this viewpoint—"My name is Snish," writes Martin, "I'm a dog. I'm a Scotty dog. Whenever the hunt comes I join in . . . ," while Susan begins, "It was a warm day and I was happily looking after my cubs. . . ." Most of the children write in the first person; some of them use only monologue—a story consisting entirely of speech-like utterances, like Martin's above. This is limiting, since it does not allow the writer to comment or shift his focus as a narrator. He is really a character in a play without the play. Others, like Susan, write a narrative in the first person—the story of a vixen and her cubs and the hunt; there is no conversation, only the events and the thoughts of a confused and frightened creature. There is little sense of writing for anyone but herself. As in dramatic play, she *is* the mother fox. Hilary, on the other hand, declares herself aware that she is writing a story in every sentence. She knows the conventions of stories, and the conventions of writing them, i.e. of punctuation and paragraphing, and she seems to enjoy it immensely. She wrote:

> The keeper opened the door of the kennels on that chilly morning. I sniffed in expectation. 'Not today chum' was all he said. I tried to make my inside do a nice deep rumble. 'No' he said, kindly but firmly—'it's the hunt! You'll enjoy that, eh boy?' I wagged my tail. 'My inside say somfin's happenin today Mum,' I said. 'You cannot,' was the prim replie 'depend on an inside, especily one like yours.' I slunk into a corner, tail between legs remembering the grass for the ponies I had chewed, 'but,' she continued, 'as it happens it is THE hunt today and you're to attend.'
>
> 'Grrrr! Gruff! Rufar! Grr! Silly old horses Grrrr.' 'Will you stop gowling!' barked an old hound, 'they help us!' I slunk away. The horn sounded and I thundered along with the others. Suddenly Canlly our champion hound picked up the scent. The horn sounded again. 'To horse! To horse!' We stampeded after fox. 'Hullo you're new' said a

friendly hound. 'First hunt' I replied proudly. 'It's great fun isn't it' he said. 'Lovely' I said 'jus' like I've always dreamed.' We streamed downhill, the wind in our faces, silky ears flapping, noses twitching but Canlly way ahead. We came to a river and stopped. Canlly sniffed uncertainly. I ventured toward him—but this was easy the scent was clear as day I bounded along after it. 'Gosh look at that pup go' said the head hunter, 'we've found another Canlly—Great!'

I was petted praised etc. After it all I said triumphantly 'well Mum even with an inside like mine you can tell a "somfin' funny day"'!

The keeper very rapidly changes his sex and turns into her mother, but the young hound triumphs and wins the argument as well. I think this story, like most of them, and like all the stories of the seven-year-olds, is really about the writer. The events—in this case a hunt—and the characters—provide the symbolic framework within which the writer makes a coherent image of a bit of life as she would like it to be.

It is interesting to see how Robert, cited earlier, feels about these matters, who was so markedly superior in his referential writing. His sympathies are all with the hounds—and these were no ordinary dogs. They were specially reared alsatians with red eyes, and the best is called Scarlet Streak. He uses the third person and writes:

The dogs barked and snarled. Then, Woddle, who was an old hand at the game, barked, jumped up high and charged forward. They had 'found' the scent. These were no ordinary dogs. They were specially reared alsatians. They all plumeted forward, knowing that the scent was that of a fox. The next five minutes were the fox's last. Knowing that he could not outrun the mighty alsatians, he crossed a stream and then crossed back to the side from which he had come. Because Woddle had first found the scent the others decided that he was shrewd and that they would follow him. Woddle, getting overconfident went over the stream. The others followed. All except Scarlet Streak. He did not see Woddle and Co. but went over another stream after the fox. After some time (1 minute) Woddle and Co followed. In one minute the fox fell, a bite through the brain.

This story is accompanied by drawings of splendid alsatians with red eyes and tongues. It is pretty much of a fairy story in spite of the sophistication of his language. Like Hilary he is aware throughout that it is the written language and a story. Every sentence declares him a reader and a confident improviser in language. What is it really about? I think it is about alsatians and the way he feels about them. I think that all the children, no less than the seven-year-olds, turn the framework of events to their own ends. Here is what Neil Hackett wrote, the only story with a sad ending; perhaps it was a story he had read. Nevertheless this is what he chose to write about. It is a different kind of hunt from all the others:

> Kotic was a seal. He had a big scar on his back. When he was two years old he was driven to the fur farm inland. One man said fire and in a few moments Kotic could not recognize any of his friends. They had all been skinned. Kotic just ran as fast as he could back to the beach but he could not. Desperately he ran round trying to get out, then a man walked up to him. Seeing the scar on Kotic's back the man flung him carelessly out of the enclosure. At that moment Kotic fainted.
>
> When he came to his senses Kotic was in great pain. He had broken his flipper. Very soon as he lay on the beach dieng he thought that men could have taken his skin anyway because they will probably take it when I am dead.

In writing about the slaughter of the seals he has distanced it somewhat. Thus it would seem that in writing their stories the children are not only exploring the possibilities of other people's and other creatures' lives, but also giving shape to aspects of their own lives, particularly their feelings.

It will be remembered that the language of the seven-year-olds' stories was very much more complex than that of their referential writing and I suggested that this was because dealing with possibilities inherent in fiction makes greater demands than dealing with simple actualities. When we come to look at this aspect of the writing of the eleven-year-olds we find a more complicated situation. First, in story writing, the children do not always choose a model which allows them to make use of the language resources that they have. The monologue is an example of this. In these cases the writers' referential pieces show more advanced forms. Second, generalization and conceptual thinking are beginning to appear in the children's referential writing and this means that they are developing forms of language that are *potentially* as powerful and complex—though different—as the language of imagination. Most children, however, do not realize this potential, and their referential writing remains a scatter of dissociated items, whereas their stories are structured by narrative form, by their feelings and by their own experience. So for most children stories (and poems) are the means by which they use language most effectively and comprehensively.

For comparison here is Neal Jackson's story together with his account of the Great Barrier Reef. It is worth noting the words he uses in each, the types of sentences demanded by the relatively simple itemized account of the Reef and the complexity of the various viewpoints he covers in his story.

The Great Barrier Reef

The 'Barrier Reef' is really little sea creatures. They are called pollyp. The Reef is on the North East coast of Australia. Often the coral forms coral islands.

These islands soon have a huge growth brought in by wood and birds.

There are many kinds and colors of coral. There is 'Stag horn', 'Dancing Lady'.

Often people go hunting on the coral and it is advised to wear pumps to safeguard against the many creatures who live in the coral.

Going back to the coral islands many creatures live there. Such as turtles who often lay a 100 to 200 eggs. When they hatch there is a mad scurry to the sea and usually only five get to the sea because of marauding birds.

The Fox Hunter

The dogs split as they came through the woods followed by about a dozen horsemen. They stumbled over a hillock squealing and barking. The dogs mostly terriers and hounds jumped over a rickerty old stone wall except for the smaller dogs who tried to find a detour.

Then everybody saw their quarry a fox. A few blows on a horn from the head hunter and the dogs split into groups. One group heading to cut the fox off by a causeway over a shallow stream. The other pack encircling the field on the fox's other side, the horsemen would cover another side and the only route opened was up a drive leading to a farm. The fox was taking a chance by trying to beat the dogs to the causeway. Somehow the fox reached the causeway and ambled over. He must have escaped.

Suddenly there was a shot which brought dog man and horse to a stop. In front of them lay the fox breathing his last breath. To the hunters right a scruffy looking farmer held a double barreled shot gun which was smoking in his arm.

'Had to get the little old critter before he got to old Bess and her little chicks.'

He turned and walked off.

The hunter blew his horn. They turned their horses and headed back the way they had come. Dogs stumbling after them.

Though in this week's work only a few poems appear, it is clear that the children read and write a good deal of poetry. The stereotyped notion of a poem as something that rhymes at all cost does not appear and the expressive language that is found in all that they write has probably the greatest scope in the poems, but there are not enough of them in the sample to make more detailed comment.

Peter wrote:

Lobo

Lobo the wolf slinking along
Lobo's feet soft and padded
But at the tip are claws of death
Which can kill a deer with one swipe
And its jawsfull of gleaming teeth
Which can break a man's backbone
You might think he's nice, out of action
But if you harm his mate watch out
because the white snarling lump of danger
will descend for the kill
You wont have time to shoot
you just try and fight with your bare hands.

It should perhaps be noted that there was in this week's work no self-initiated writing as there was in the work from the seven-year-olds. With the eleven-year-olds all that they wrote arose from a common experience, from which they pursued their own directions. We do not therefore know whether the common starting point in the literature read that week *provided scope* for the children's preoccupations which they would not otherwise have found, or whether the theme of the hunt *prevented* some of them from writing about preferred areas of experience. What is clear is that Alan Brownjohn's poem "To See the Rabbit" produced several imitations so close to the original that they seemed to have little relation to the children's own experience. This raises the question of whether referential and spectator writing might not have different starting points. The referential must at some point work towards that which is held in common. This would seem never to be the need in spectator writing which realizes the individual's satisfaction as a "maker." Literature is clearly of crucial importance, but perhaps it should not be too near to the children's writing in time, or too directly linked by the teacher to what they are about to write.

C. The Nine-year-olds: A Week's Work

The school

The work of this class came from 26 children, 11 boys and 15 girls aged nine to ten in a Primary school in an industrial town of 50,000 inhabitants. The town expanded from a village in the 1920's, so that much of the housing is modern (post-1920), but few of the children's parents have any roots in the place; they have come, over the years, from Scotland and the North of England to work in the new industries. The school itself is the old village school, a pre-World War I building situated near the industrial zone. It is old-fashioned in that it has a fixed time-table for lessons, much formal instruction, a good deal of copying of material and set exercises, and there is in this class no extended work based on firsthand experience, and little opportunity for self-chosen writing or other work. The teacher of this class was probably the most informal in the school. Each year-group of the school is streamed into three classes, of which this is one of the two lower ones.

The writings

Each child in this class had done 25 to 30 items and a good many crayon pictures, but their books were very much school exercise books, with a fair sprinkling of red ink corrections. There was no sense, as there was with the eleven-year-olds, of something made, and mounted and illustrated. The books contained a great deal of scrappy, non-continuous writing such as word lists, spelling lists, answers to questions given orally, items set out in numbered sentences (e.g. How Jesus turned the water into wine), and half a page of arithmetic—just figures, meaningless as they appear in the books. At any point between these items poems appeared, copied or made up, between 6 and 10 of these in most books. Between 10 and 12 of the items were concerned with the work the children were doing that week on telling the time. This included making a clock face with movable hands, answering questions every day about time, one piece of continuous informational writing about ways of telling time in the past, and poems about clocks.

In addition to this work on "time" and all the other miscellaneous exercises, there were 5 pieces of continuous writing which all the children did; all these were directly related to work done in lessons. They were:

1. How you got in touch with someone by telephone;
2. A report of a radio lesson on how we hear sounds together with drawings of the structure of the ear;
3. An imagined account of travel in Tudor times;
4. How Jesus calmed the waves;
5. The reproduction of a fable about the sun and the wind.

Over and above all the directed work (some 670 items for the class as a whole), there were 8 pieces of self-chosen writing—4 brief accounts of personal experiences and 4 stories—and in addition, 8 children copied out items of information which interested them.

It needs to be noted that there was almost no self-chosen work in the class discussed in Section B (eleven-year-olds), in that almost everything they wrote arose from some common starting point: i.e. their writing was also related to work done in lessons. But, given a common starting point they then diverged in 34 different directions even when the starting point was an informational one. I have suggested that these divergences arose from the teacher's expectation that they would pursue their own individual lines of enquiry and that with this in mind they were provided with a rich and varied matrix of common experience to start from. In the class now under discussion, among the items (1 to 5) listed above, only items 1 and 3 allowed the children to take individual directions within narrow limits; the other three demanded a set pattern of events—sheer reproduction in fact.

If we ask the same question that we asked before—what are these children doing in their writing?—we have to reply that in most of their work they are reproducing things that they have learned in their lessons, showing their teacher that they have learned them. Richard summarizes it for us:

> when we where having lessons this morning we lernt about time and we lernd about a.m. and p.m. and that am is in the morning and pm menes in the after-noon. and we have lernt time-table time and that clock wise mens the same way as the clock gows and anti clockwise mines the opposite way to the clock.

Since most of the writing of this class is very near to speech, perhaps the most useful way of looking at it will therefore be to try to trace the points at which it moves away towards other models.

The seven-year-olds and the eleven-year-olds were given opportunity and encouragement in verbalizing their individual experiences—their day-to-day living, their fantasy and their new experiences arising from work at school. Out of all the writing done by these nine-year-olds (Class C) there were only *four* pieces concerned with personal experience. Two were about visits to the circus; here is one of them. Senga wrote:

> One day daddy came home with four tickets for the circus. daddy are we going to the circus I said yes we all are said daddy we are going to night. Oh goody goody I said. we all better get ready now my mummy said So off we went. At the circus people where coming in and sitting down, then a lady said the trapeze boys It was good fun looking at them next it was red nose the clown with his pet monkey He was very funny the circus was good I said and my mummy said it was good too.

This is very like the way she would speak and is very little shaped by a sense of the occasion: there is more focus on the events leading up to the circus than on the circus itself. It is expressive and carries a sense of her feelings about the whole situation.

Here is another of the four pieces, written by Linda Cummings:

Play Time

I went to see if my friend was coming out to play with me and so I went to see If she was coming out She was coming out so we had a game of hide and seek together and then my mummy said come in and get your tea and then I had to go to the shop for my mum and she gave me sixpence to spend and then I came home and I went out to play again I played shopping with my friend and I had to go in because my Mum said and then I had to watch television for an hour and then I had to go to bed.

This, like the previous one, is structured only by the sequence of events as they happened. It is much nearer the writing of the seven-year-olds in general than it is to that of the eleven-year-olds in general. This is written down speech with the elements connected by "and" and "then." If this piece of Linda's is put alongside the story by Nicola, aged seven, on p. 71 and also alongside the piece by Lyn, aged eleven, *A Few Days in the Garden* on p. 81, we can now see at all three age levels the most elementary form of the written language being used; if there were no other work to look at it would be difficult to guess the ages of these three children. But both the older children *can* use other modes, though Lyn from Class B, with a rich school experience and much feed-in from literature does not go beyond speech models as yet (her piece about Pond Life is quoted on p. 81). Linda at nine (from Class C) and with much more limited opportunities for varied writing can move into another mode, though it looks as if her work in general is well beneath her capabilities because of the restricted nature of the curriculum. Here is what she wrote about travel in Tudor times:

In the Tudor days more of the people *travelled about towns* on horseback and the roads were very bumpy and very bad. The farmers took big heavy stones out of the roads and there was big holes as well . . . The king and the queen *spent much of their time* going round the country. *When it was known* the king and queen were visiting towns folk they hurried very very very quickly to mend there roads and queen Elizabeth had more waggons than anyone. She had for hundred waggons all together when she went on her journeys.

Here is a mixture of her own speech model beginning to be modified by the teacher's language and possibly by books. Her writing here has moved towards the referential.

The rest of the writings in Linda's book are either exercises or reproductions so she had no other chances to try her hand at real writing, no opportunity to use her own language to help her learning.

If we now look at the four stories we find that three of them are about mysterious or alarming night occurrences. They are brief and have moved only marginally towards the poetic—they begin and end as stories might be expected to do. For example Timothy wrote:

A Scare

One night on a Friday at 12 o'clock I was very thirsty so I got up for a drink of water and heard a scream so I went to my bedroom window and I saw a big man with a beg on his back it was a burgaw. So I called 999 for the police. . . .

There follows another paragraph of the same length in which the police catch the burglar. But Linda Harman wrote a different kind of story which is reproduced in full for several reasons. It is not written down speech. Linda has a sense that she is writing a story and it is the only clear instance of this in the whole class. She knows some of the conventions of the written language—full stops and capital letters, for instance, and the way she uses dialogue shows some influence from children's stories of the Enid Blyton type.

The Things that Jane and Sally saw

When Jane and Sally woke up the curtains where drawn back and the sun was shining in the bedroom. 'O' look at the sun it is as bright as as every said Jane and Sally. Just then there mummy came in. Mummy mummy look at the sun it is ever so shiney. Yes I no said mummy. What have you got in your hands said Jane. "O" yes I have been up the shops when you where sleeping and bort you a new dress each. Can we wear them today said Sally. Yes said mummy that's how I have brought them up.When there Mummy showd them the dress that she had bought them they said 'O' they are very nice said Jane and Sally and they put them on. Are you ready said there mother. Yes gust coming said Jane and Sally. 'O' you look pretty said there mother. Where going for a walk before we go to school. What do you want to go for a walk for. Our teacher told us to try and get some flowers for the classroom. Well you havn't got time to go to the woods so you can go round the farm to see if you can find some flowers there. So Jane and Sally went out to look for some flowers in there farm. When they got out of the house, all they could see was long green grass and lose of pretty flowers. 'O' aren't they lovely said Jane. 'O' yes they are the most lovelyes flowers I have ever seen said Sally. There was roses and daisies daffodils and lilys and tulips and panseys. Jane and Sally took 5 each of the flowers. Then there mother came out it is time for school so off they went. When the teacher saw them she said thank you and put them in water.

This is, I think, a fantasy in spite of its seeming to be concerned with realistic things such as new dresses and flowers for the teacher. I suggest it is an arrangement of imagined events as Linda would like them to be—a shadowy friend who can scarcely be distinguished from the writer, a new dress, praise (how pretty you look), being allowed to pick the best flowers from the garden, the teacher's gratitude. So, in this respect, Linda is doing in her story what all the other writers were doing, making a satisfactory pattern from imagined events, rearranging life as it might be, and this, of course, is what professional story writers do too. Judging by the rest of the work in the children's books—though it is easy to misjudge in having only the books to look at—she has not been encouraged to express her own responses to things, so she has fallen back on this particular literary model with its stereotyped and unexpressive dialogue—another case of starved capabilities. Compare this with seven-year-old Mary's account of the incident with Mrs. Bowaller on p. 67. It is significant that this story of Linda Harman's is the longest piece written by any of the Class C children, with one exception which I shall come to later. Children need enough opportunities to write stories—and need enough stories to read—for them to develop the sense (which the seven-year-olds so clearly had) that a story is something "out there," something made. In this class, this story—dull though it seems—is the only one which exhibits this sense, but there were only four written. In order to compare the work of this class with that of the other two classes I have had to focus on the four pieces of any length and quality. A survey of the whole range of work is more conclusively revealing than the individual examples I have quoted.

Although there is little evidence of prose literature in the children's writing there are many poems scattered about in their books. Some of these are copied and some are made up but it is clear that although they like the poems that they copy—many have illustrated them for instance—the poems that they write are no more than word games in which the need to find rhymes drives out sense. For instance, Steven writes:

I went to bed
And saw a man
He had a pram
And he had a red thing on his head.

I went under my cover
Because I though he was a goast
And I told my brother
And he had some toast.

And John wrote:

I go to school every day
And I want to play

And it was the middle of may
And that was the end of the day.

All of them are like this, so the poems that they write are not expressions of felt experience. One could contrast with these the poem Lobo on p. 90.

There remains for comment only the copied pieces. Most of these are about what one might expect—types of airplane, inspection pits in a garage, a bus conductor's ticket machine, Roman bridges, Christopher Columbus, items that may reflect the children's interests or merely some available material to copy; they are all brief except one, and this one stands out by its length and by the fact that the boy kept it up during three days, writing it before and after the interruptions that his set work clearly constitutes. The handwriting is beautiful and it occupies five full pages, much the greatest amount that anyone wrote. It is the only language of quality and imagination (including the poems) that can be found in all the books. Here is part of it:

Wasps

The Buzzing can be heard in gardens and fields in summer time and autumn. The wasps are looking for nectar in the flowers. They settle on fruit in the orchards and suck the sweet juice. Bees may be flying there too. The wasps are a brighter yellow and smoother than the bees. . . . The wasp has two very large eyes. On her head also are two long black feelers. With these she can smell and feel her way about . . . Only the queen lives through the cold winter. She sleeps or hibernates in a sheltered place. It may be the bark of a tree or under some dry leaves. On a warm day in spring the queen wasp wakes. She crawls out into the sunshine and spreads her wings. She feeds on nectar from the flowers. Then she looks round for somewhere to build a new nest. The queen wasp may find a hole left by a field mouse or a mole. . . .

and so on to the end of the cycle of life of the wasp. Judging only on what is in the children's books, starvation of imagination is hardly too strong a term to use: beside such a diet this piece is a rich feast. One other boy also copied part of this passage.

To summarize the chief differences between the writings of this class and those of the other two classes: Most of the writing is discontinuous—lists, sentences, etc.; there is a lack of firsthand experience, and no attempt to get the children to use their own language to explore new experience; there is little impact from literature and an absence of imaginative writing of any sort; they have very little opportunity of choice since so much of their writing is closely tied to recapitulating information from lessons. It is quite likely that the social environment is less favorable than that of the other two classes, but we know from evidence from other schools where the children from homes with limited backgrounds that exploration of the physical environment at first hand can result in writing of a quality and quantity which does not begin to be reached by these children. Expressive work hardly appears in these books; there is much incoherent and non-continuous referential writing, and there is little movement towards the poetic.

But there is a postscript.

A set of large paintings came in as part of the week's work. These arose from class discussion about the relative costs and advantages of different kinds of transport, and each child had written a few lines about his picture on a square of lined paper and stuck it on one corner. While this rather spoiled the paintings it also allowed them to have an effect on the writing, and because the pictures were much more directly related to firsthand experience than was the class discussion, a little crop of expressive and imaginative writings appeared on the stuck-on slips; for example:

I am the Driver of a big plane . . . it is very hard when we go up through a cloud and it is very hard work when we land as well. . . .

I am a fruit lady and I go around the doors selling my fruit

One day my daddy gave me a ride in a car transporter. . . .

My dad works in Golden Wonder. He drives a lorry load of crisps. . . . But my dad gets a good wage. He likes the job.

I'm moving today Hurray Hurray
The time has come today
I'm moving today Hurray Hurray
I'm moving to Scotland today today.

I have tried in this study to draw out, from a detailed examination of all the written work done in one particular week, some very general points about children's language; but the writings that form the sample can only give a partial picture and the study is not intended as a critical comparison of teaching methods in the three classes, though any such study implies consideration of the teaching in the background.

The question, "What are children up to in their writing?" implies, of course, that children do not write just to practice writing. At one level they are simply cooperating with their teachers—doing what they are asked to do, but over and above this, they seem to be engaged on the one hand in handling *information*, reporting things about the world around, sometimes in their own terms and sometimes in language taken over from their teachers or from books; on the other hand they seem to be using their writing to improvise upon experience for the fun of doing so, to explore the possibilities of experience, to enjoy—that is to say—experience they have not had. These two directions in their writing correspond to the distinction that James Britton makes between language in the role of spectator, which he defines as one of the characteristics of literature, and language in the role of participant which is language used for some practical end. Clearly one kind often shades into the other, especially in the writing of younger children, but the striking difference between their stories and all their other writing suggests a difference in function arising from a different relationship between the writer and his situation. The children's accounts of preferences for pets or football teams, of how we hear sounds or of how Jesus calmed the waves were for the purpose of reporting and recording and explaining, whereas their stories were symbolic representation of their inner preoccupations and interests. The distinction is important because it enables us to see how literature and personal and imaginative writing on the one hand, and writing that is concerned with knowledge in its generally accepted sense on the other, are complementary, and that both need to be fostered. The importance of participant writing is self-evident; children cannot advance in school education without it. The importance of language in the role of spectator is not so obvious because it is not directly related to practical ends. Yet in terms of its function in children's development it can be seen to be of the utmost importance.

Within the writing in the spectator mode we find both autobiographical and fictional (or fantasy) stories. The first are important because they establish the validity of children's own experience now, for themselves and in the eyes of their teachers; this is the creative milieu. The second—the area of fantasy—is the only mode by which children can give utterance to areas of experience which are most powerful but which they cannot be explicit about—their fears, anxieties, griefs, hopes, excitements and preoccupations. These can only be represented symbolically and this is what the stories are really about. Sometimes the characters are mothers and fathers and boys and girls, sometimes animals, sometimes farmers or shopkeepers or taximen, sometimes old men or witches or giants—the disguise is significant—and the "persons" and events play out the concerns of the writers. Fantasy, whether expressed in dramatic play or in stories or pictures, is the only mode open to young children to interpret their most powerful experiences. Blake says,

> The child's toys and the old man's reasons
> Are the fruit of the two seasons.

Yet the power of fantasy never ceases to surprise. Vygotsky's comment that the motives for writing are often far from children is, I think, true for writing in the role of participant. Writing to report or argue or explain often looms as a task, but fantasy has its roots in emotion and dream and is powerful enough to overcome the physical labor of writing and the distractions of angry adults calling for attention and action. Furthermore, the scope of stories makes possible all sorts of extension of language, and the writing of children with experience of literature reflects these extensions.

It seems appropriate to end with a story which embodies most of the theoretical ideas expressed in this article. Stephen Tolley wrote a letter to a visiting teacher to explain why his work was late. He is eleven and in his first term in his secondary school. He wrote:

Dear Mrs. Smith

My monster is late because I did not finish it in English and I only had a cuple of lines to do and I finished it off in geography so my house tutor mister mordred taw it up and I had to take it home and do it. I hope you like it from Stephen Tolley yours faithily.

With the letter came his "monster"—the second one, which he had done at home. The middle of the page was a picture of a visionary monster with flames shooting from his scaly purple head and a "long strong" orange tail. Above and below the picture was his story. The picture was not an illustration; the picture and the story round it was a construct of imagination; the words said:

Fier Cali

He has rough hard scales like a crocodiles on his head, a body like a great lizard and legs like a dragon and a long strong tail. He has butiful coulers and he breafees out flames. I once went into a cave with a river running through. I did not know about the monster I just walked in. I saw a flame round a bend and I was practically paralised. When I saw the monster I turned and ran as fast as possible. I was speechless but I went back again.

by
Stephen T.

His regular English teacher said about the incident:

Anyway Stephen cried and wouldn't really be consoled by 5:30 p.m. when I saw him. However I gave him a stamped addressed envelope so that he can do it again if he wants to.

Stephen's letter is a piece of writing with a practical aim. Its function is to explain why his work was not done. It is also, I think, to maintain his relationship with the new teacher. It is participant writing because he wants it to affect the course of events.

His "monster" as he calls it—his construct of imagination—has no such practical purpose. He had accepted the teacher's request to write about a monster and had made the task his own. From then on, its purpose lay in the satisfaction of making it, and in his assumption that the teacher would share his satisfaction—this is language in the role of spectator.

8

Language Across the Curriculum:

A Paradox and Its Potential for Change

Abstract

This paper gives some account of the outcomes of the Schools Council project Writing Across the Curriculum 11–16, *but is primarily concerned with theoretical problems of the relationships between teaching, research and development in language. One of the most far-reaching changes envisaged by the Bullock Committee is to be found in its recommendation that all teachers should take responsibility for the language development of their students not only in their specialist areas but, in conjunction with other teachers, for language policies across the whole curriculum. Yet to arrive at a policy for language means asking fundamental questions about learning, and teaching, and this can only be done by the various subject specialists who do not generally regard themselves as concerned with language.*

Introduction

There are a number of things that particularly interest me in this Project, which strictly speaking is concerned with *writing* across the secondary curriculum. They are essentially theoretical matters because the problems are new and therefore demand new solutions. The problems are there because this Project is not a *subject* project; yet secondary schools are organized on a subject-basis. This is the first paradoxical element. For the same reasons, development in language across the curriculum is not susceptible to direct application, as might be for instance *Mathematics for the Majority* or

Paper given at Jerome Bruner's fifth Language and Learning seminar at Oxford, January, 1975; published in *Educational Review*, Vol. 28, No. 3, June, 1976.

Geography for the Young School Leaver. It has to be approached through the looking glass, as it were. Secondly, its potential for change seems enormous, because it is not an accumulation of teachers each separately attempting to do something about language in their subjects, though it is this too, but it is also the potentially explosive matter of teachers drawing out their own and other teachers' purposes—and practices—and examining them *together.* When this happens among equals (or near-equals even in the school hierarchies) and voluntarily, for an exploratory and not an immediately didactic purpose, the potential for change is of a different order from that initiated by any outsiders. I quote in illustration the case of a physics teacher whose lesson was taped and transcribed by one of the Project Officers. The teacher subsequently offered a transcript of this lesson as discussion material for a number of the staff to discuss with reference to their attempts to formulate a language policy for the school. Since you cannot be *seriously* concerned about language without being concerned with learning, what is really happening is a review of learning. So, it is the dynamics of this development Project that seem to me of particular interest; and which may have greater general significance than one can as yet perceive from inside. My hypothesis is that the tension between contradictory elements is the dynamic of change.

The Project and its Aims

In 1971 the Schools Council funded the Writing Across the Curriculum Project 11–16 to:

1. disseminate the theory and the findings of the five-year research into the development of writing abilities;
2. assist teachers to explore in their work the possibilities arising from a more informed understanding of the role of writing (and talking) in school learning;
3. help teachers to develop language policies across the curriculum in their schools.

In short, there were things teachers of all subjects ought to know about language in schools, and there were things they could do about it if they knew. So our aim was twofold, to disseminate certain information, and to persuade teachers to innovate in the light of the usefulness of this information to them. We were not, therefore, so much concerned with the direct application of research, but with the new hypotheses that teachers would make in terms of their own subjects and particular educational stances.

Theoretical Perspectives

Our dissemination of the findings of the Writing research was based on that research's background of language learning theory (Britton et al.

1975). From this perspective we saw the development of writing abilities not so much in terms of the acquisition of varying skills as of a hierarchy of kinds of writing shaped by the thinking problems which the writer encountered. Our focus was, therefore, on the relationship of school writing to learning. Most previous research in our field did not take account of differentiated writing. Some earlier research (Britton, Martin, Rosen, 1966) showed that at 16 the *kind* of writing a school student chose to do made a big difference to his examination mark; i.e. writing is not a "global" ability, and some kinds of writing are easier than others and are acquired earlier. In our study of the development of writing abilities we surveyed the kinds of writing done in schools across the curriculum, and tried to trace a pattern of development in the ability to move into different kinds of writing. We defined progress (for our purposes) in terms of this increasing capacity to differentiate. In the event we found a narrowing, both by function and audience, as pupils went up the secondary school: the predicted differentiation did not generally take place.

The theoretical perspectives of our second and third aims are much more tenuous. A development project has too often been seen as the direct application of research findings to school situations, i.e. a model of application has been borrowed from the natural sciences or technology. Indeed, we ourselves began our actual work in this way by going into schools for six weeks and hoping to make observable changes in the written outcomes by changing this or that in the context according to our research model of discourse. Subsequent discussion of what was implied by this way of working led us to set up a different theoretical model of a development project which took account of innovative processes more generally, that is to say in teachers and also in their pupils. We drew on Halsey's notion of action-research in the Social Sciences. He says: "Where Projects have little clear knowledge about how objectives are to be reached, the research approach as we have outlined it is either ineffective, . . . or it turns the action away from exploration. . . . In the more effective projects the emphasis of research is not purely on outcomes but is also on the processes that take place during the project. . . ." (Halsey 1972, p. 177) And we drew on James Britton's exploration of the relationships between teaching, research and development in a paper with that title (Britton 1970). He writes: "Putting it crudely, it is the continual reformulation of what we know in the light of what we perceive that matters: and the hardening of what we know into a formula that we apply ready-made instead of reformulating—that is the danger. Thus, our most powerful ideas are relatively general, relatively unformulated starting points from which we constantly reformulate.

"Research findings are things we can *know* which could have a bearing on what we *do* when we teach. And 'development' should be the name we give to the process of bringing this kind of knowing into relationship with this kind of doing. But how does it work?

"The conclusion reached by a research team working in controlled situations cannot be directly apprehended and applied by teachers working in conditions where every variable is actively varying. . . .

"For development is a two-way process: the practitioner does not merely *apply;* he must reformulate from the general starting points supplied by the research and arrive at new ends—new not only to him, but new in the sense that they are not a part of the research findings, being a discovery of a different order."

Thus we saw the relationship between research and teaching as the re-hypothesizing of research findings by teachers in the light of the meanings built up from their past experiences; and the assessment of the outcomes would also rest with them when set against their educational aims and purposes in teaching their various subjects. Furthermore, as Halsey predicted, the directions and attitudes of the Project team have been influenced by the various operations and stages of our work and, of course, by the people we have worked with.

Special Problems of This Project

The Project has two particular problems: (1) it is concerned with language *across the curriculum* in secondary schools, and the general pattern of the organization of secondary schools works against it; the social structure and autonomous status arising from this subject specialist type of organization makes even talking together about language by teachers of different subjects a problem. They could do this but it seems they seldom do. Apart from pressures of time there are implicit assumptions that a specialist will be able to manage his own affairs—including, of course, the language proper to his subject. (2) This problem is compounded by the fact that most secondary teachers (other than some teachers of English) think of language as something to be corrected and improved. So our starting aims were to get people to recognize it as a major intellectual tool, and go on to examine the part language—and in particular writing—played in the teaching of their subjects. In effect, this meant a shift of focus from how they viewed language to how they viewed learning.

What is at issue here is a means-ends debate. Most subject teachers realize that language is a means to learning. The shortfall in their view is a failure to realize its potential. The Bullock Report (in spite of Chapter IV, Language and Learning) treats it, on the whole, as an *end,* as do very many English and remedial teachers. Unless a focus is kept on its potential for learning, the campaigns for language policies and "establishing teachers' involvement in language and reading development throughout the years of schooling" may settle into a drive for surface features only and a great opportunity may slip away.

The problem, of course, is not just one of language. It is an aspect of the sociology of knowledge. Basil Bernstein analyzes the general problem in his paper on *The Classification and Framing of Classroom Knowledge* (Bernstein 1971) and discusses the implications of subject boundaries on school organization, teacher status, institutional "messages," teacher-pupil relationships and the way these affect the implicit and explicit language policies that schools actually operate.

In this context the position of the Project team was as follows: As research workers and subject specialists (two English, one geography) we could with confidence offer our research findings and their implications for school learning and language; and we could expect these to be discussed. And these expectations were fulfilled. More than this, we could offer advice to English and geography teachers about what they might *do* in their classrooms. What we could not do was tell other specialists what they might do in their classrooms. It looked at first as if the contradictions between our brief—language across the curriculum—and the "classification and framing" of subject knowledge in schools might defeat the enterprise.

But it's an ill wind etc. . . . We had observed that innovations in schools which are the result of a new theoretical position tend to be taken up as if they were just an alternative *method,* and the theoretical implications which could have more far-reaching results get lost. This is the force of Britton's point about our most powerful ideas being relatively general, relatively unformulated starting points from which we constantly reformulate. It is these powerful general ideas which tend to get lost when Project teams have the remit of "surveying good practice" and disseminating it, i.e. when they are in a position to advise teachers what to do in their classrooms. We could not do this: we had to begin by asking teachers what they did, and this created a fundamentally different situation. We asked them, for instance, what use they made of talk, and how they saw its function in learning; what they set writing for and whether they saw it as having any role in helping children to think etc. etc. In short, by being forced to start by asking questions (real questions, not loaded ones) we and the teachers soon found ourselves asking "why?," i.e. what are the education purposes of doing whatever you do in history, for instance, and what is the part that language plays in this? We have thus been enabled by circumstances—as well as design—to focus our work on teachers' views of learning in the first place and secondly, on language in relation to it.

Of course methodology came into it. Teachers were interested in the outcomes from other teachers' lessons, but the discussions never rested there. They always came back to the question, "What do *you* do? and why?"

There was, however, another facet to our work. Part of our brief has been to try to persuade teachers to develop language *policies* for their schools, that is, a consciously formulated policy for language development and reading worked out in discussion between different members of staff—

across the curriculum. The implications of this seem very great, and the precedents nil. Government Reports are generally addressed to organizing bodies and individuals; each is expected to operate as best he can in his particular sphere. Of course discussions have gone on as the result of the Newsome, the Plowden, the Crowther Reports, but classroom action taken has been by individuals. If Recommendation 4 of the Bullock Report means anything, it must mean consultation, revision and reformulation by groups of teachers as school personnel changes and educational events occur. This already happens in some schools and not at all in others. What is new is the recommendation that a policy for language should be *deliberate* and *organized* and *across the curriculum.*

What Has Been Happening in the Classrooms, Among Teachers, and in the Schools

In trying to assess what has been happening, we have drawn on observations from three sources: our own interpretations and analyses of teachers' innovations; children's observations about writing, about language, about learning, about assessment (transcripts of conversations); teachers' perceptions and observations about these matters and of their own practices (transcripts and writings).

In the classrooms. With this multiple monitoring process as a background we have presented certain theoretical ideas and research findings in our discussion pamphlets together with some of the outcomes from schools—transcripts of lessons, for instance, and conversations and student writings—always in the contexts from which they came. Essentially these writings illustrate more reflective roles for writing as against the dominant role of test or record found in our previous research survey. Quite dramatic changes have occurred when teachers have widened the audience to include peer groups or the writer himself, or when students have been invited to reflect on their learning *without assessment.*

Among teachers. We have worked on the principle that it is more effective for people to experience things than be told about them; so we have usually arranged workshop sessions at meetings and conferences. In these, everyone, including the Project team, has been in learning situations, such as doing practical experiments in science (surface tension, or soil testing for example), history worksheets based on resource material, various writing tasks. Much of these sessions were tape-recorded and then discussed. By engaging teachers in their own learning situations they could recognize the problems in themselves.

In schools. In the last year we have shifted our focus of attention in courses and meetings to include planning sessions for teachers' follow-up action in their own schools—or in meetings with neighboring schools. This has involved discussion of the practical problems of who to approach, the attitudes of head and senior staff, possibilities of meetings between members of different departments, what issues need to be discussed, what outcomes could be expected. This whole area has proved by far the most difficult. It seems to represent totally new procedures for many teachers, and the simplest step has needed a great deal of discussion.

What Is Now Emerging

We observed that the examples of children's written and spoken language which reflects individual thinking came from single students or the pupils of small groups of teachers who were interested in our research and made use of it. They have not generally represented the work of a whole class—or even the majority in a class—let alone a whole school. We have therefore begun to suspect that the changes we have found are exceptions or isolated cases. We think these children were probably already committed to learning and therefore responded very positively to enlarged opportunities. We think the majority of children remain generally uncommitted.

If this is right it means that special programs for this or that will have little effect. We need to start further back and work on the problem of getting more pupils involved in their work and this means taking more account of their intentions. Most teachers are concerned about what they generally call "motivation," but it is usually seen in short-term contexts—how to get them interested in this or that piece of work, i.e. persuading them to accept the teacher's intention. We suggest that as long as our gaze is almost exclusively on language—as is the Bullock Committee's—the teachers' intentions and the children's intentions will seldom coincide. "For the intentions which pupils have that can lead them into language acts are not intentions about language but about 'content'—that is, about *something:* thing, idea, memory, feeling, fantasy, image, book, that they want to tell someone about or find out from someone about. So to arrive at some useful ideas on how to get the intentions happening it would be necessary to give some thought to the world of 'what is talked about'." (Medway 1975, p. 67) Language in action cannot be separated from what it is used for and with what intent, and whose intent.

This hypothesis suggests that every piece of writing, and the circumstances that gave rise to it, represents a network of past experience, relationships and expectations linked to a continuum of other such networks. In what follows we have attempted to identify what seem to us to be emerging as the most significant features in these webs of learning and language. But, as we would now expect, the items which we see as significant are themselves networks. This interrelatedness throws light on why efforts by individual teachers to make a change here or a change there have only resulted in what we have referred to as "isolated cases" of progress. We think changes have to be more wide-spreading to be effective.

Enabling/Disabling Features in Contexts for Learning and Language

How a learner sees himself. His view of himself as a school student depends a great deal on how his teachers see him. How his teachers respond to his effort, or lack of effort, depends in turn upon how the teacher sees *himself,* and his view of his role as a teacher is closely related to his view of learning. When we look at language in these contexts we find the kinds of experience and of language reckoned appropriate to the classroom is closely related to the teacher's view of learning and his role relationships to his pupils.

A writer's sense of audience. We think it likely that one reason for the great amount of inert, inept writing produced by school students is that the natural process of internalizing the sense of audience, learned through speech, has been perverted by the use of writing as a testing or reproductive procedure at the expense of all other functions of writing.

Assessment and criticism. The most dramatic changes in writing that we observed came when teachers moved out of their role as examiner into the role of an adult consultant. The unresolved problem remains—at what points in children's engagement in the process of writing do advice and criticism assist rather than divert? Medway and Goodson attempt to analyze the phases in children's involvement in classroom writing and the different levels of teacher intervention in a seminal article published by this Project (Medway and Goodson 1975) but work in this area is thin on the ground.

The role of everyday language in learning. The things we choose to put into words, and the words which come to hand to express these meanings, reflect our unique interpretations of experience. We need to *begin* by accepting—and encouraging—children's own language whatever it may be. Particularly in the written language this view collides with notions of standard English. This is usually debated out of the context of varying classroom activities involving language, and has little to do with the central position of language as an intellectual tool.

Conditions for moving into good transactional writing. The written language in its transactional form dominates the secondary school curriculum (Britton et al. 1975). Because of its importance as a vehicle of ideas, and because of its difficulty, one of the major aims of the Project has been to try to track down good transactional writing by pupils and use these written utterances as points of departure for analysis of the situations from which they came—to identify the enabling or disabling features of these situations, and what part language played in the whole complex (Martin et al. 1976). We have come up with two conditions which were always present in our case studies of successful transactional writing, though the interrelatedness of all the features we have attempted to identify suggest that these conditions themselves depend on others:

The interplay of firsthand and secondary experience. In firsthand experience we would include the student's reflections on the operations or information he has been working with. In short, while a learner he needs to be at the center of his own learning.

There should be opportunities for students to encounter good and varied models of trnasactional language—to be encountered rather than imitated. Often such models are limited to a single textbook.

Changes in notions of progress in learning and language. In a series of seminars with science teachers we were constantly brought back to a consideration of creative thinking and creativity. With a comparable group of humanities teachers the central issue was cooperative learning. We see these as closely related, and also related negatively to the constraints on intention and choice which arise from general secondary school procedures. We don't think it entirely accidental that these two particular issues arose so persistently. This is what the hypotheses and findings of the Writing research point towards, though it only became apparent as the ideas were realized in the work coming from classrooms. If intention is the motivating force for thinking as well as action, then creativity in a very general sense would seem to be related to intention. If we could then accept some kind of balance between the teachers' intentions (programs, syllabuses, etc.) and those of the pupils, we should have something like co-operative learning/teaching.

We think these notions might be important in getting more children to commit themselves to learning. We also think that for such commitment to happen on a wider scale than our observed isolated cases, whole environments for learning may need to be changed. For this to happen we think there would have to be enough teachers in a school who shared a view about learning and language to create a different set of possibilities in the school. We know two secondary schools and one middle school where this is beginning to happen.

To return, in conclusion, to our third aim, assistance to teachers in formulating agreed language policies across the curriculum. We refer to three documents which indicate the kind of steps that are being taken, and also the vast educational scope of the enterprise:

From a Middle School in County Durham. A "Statement of Intent" which had been produced from many discussions between the headmaster and "teaching staff who were to be the nucleus of a larger and changing staff of the new Middle School." A rider was added that if any teacher having joined the staff was unable to accept the underlying educational philosophy of the "Statement" they should discuss this with the headmaster so that an "acceptable solution to the dilemma" could be found. Accompanying this "Statement of Intent" was a document headed "The Language Policy of a School." This document went with a video tape of a mixed ability class aged 12–13 filmed throughout three days and covering all the activities that this class engaged in, all lessons, including drama, P.E., craft, Library, taking Assembly, having school dinner, etc. The Language Policy document is meant to be seen as part of the school objectives and contains 11 aims. The first sentence reads: "We hope that the video tape-recording will illustrate as many of the following points as possible." Clearly such a way of producing a language policy involved all the staff, disposed of the notorious gap between statements of objectives and actual practice, opened all the practices to public discussion, and located the language policy firmly in the more general aims of the school.

We report here the second stage in an attempt by a group of teachers in a London comprehensive school to get a language policy going. It is headed "Language across the curriculum at Thomas Calton School, 2nd report, February 1976." The first sentence reads: "Since the first report in May last year (1975) our efforts have been directed towards producing a questionnaire for the school's various subject departments. . . ." We have only space to quote some of it:

- To what extent can your department help in the teaching of reading?
- Can your department make more use of work in small groups?
- Can your department make more use of talk as part of the learning process?
- What attitude does your department have to non-standard English in speech and writing?
- How much does the work of your department encourage teachers to talk to individual pupils?
- Are we asking for too narrow a range of writing from our pupils. . . .?
- What sorts of assignments should we set to produce the most effective *learning* situations?

". . . this is an enormous undertaking and the truth is that when we make statements about language we often expose the heart of our educational philosophy. . . . These questions which are an attempt to communicate with the rest of the staff . . . were devised by those who attended the two meetings. . . . It should also be remembered that each school situation is unique, and what may be relevant in our school may be actually harmful in another."

Our final document comes from an anonymous teacher working, like others, at setting down his individual first steps in doing something about a language policy in his school:

"*School situation:* small (500) rural grammar school, joining with local secondary modern school (at present half-mile away, 400 children) to form one-site comprehensive. Traditional approaches to most subjects. Little will to innovate (from top downwards).

Possible Follow-up:

1. Report back to Head, emphasizing Bullock. Ask permission to make following moves:
2. Begin arrangement of meeting (with two neighboring schools) for Science or Maths teacher (outsider) to describe his attitudes.
3. Talk to own department (English) and describe course. Ask for follow-up suggestions since they have all been in the school longer than I have.
4. Approach those members of other departments with whom I have already had 'education' talk. Ask how they view English (ought I to say 'Language'?) in school.
5. Get them to complete questionnaire—possibly criticizing work of English department.
6. Collate these remarks and invite contributors to meet and discuss their views."

It is noticeable that these teachers, like the Project team, had to begin by asking *questions* of their colleagues, and that the questions led them into educational purposes. Educational purposes are various, so language policies will also vary, not only from school to school, but from time to time in the same school. So we come back to James Britton's formulation of the relationship between teaching, research and development. "Development is a two-way process: the practitioner does not merely *apply:* he must reformulate from the general starting points supplied by the research and arrive at new ends . . . the value of each discovery is limited to the successful solution of this particular problem at this particular time; but the power of the teacher to make that journey and make it again—there above all lies the value of the whole enterprise."

References

Basil Bernstein. "The Classification and Framing of Classroom Knowledge," in M. F. D. Young, *Knowledge and Control.* Collier Macmillan, 1971.

James Britton, Nancy Martin and Harold Rosen. *The Multiple Making of English Composition.* HMSO, 1966.

James Britton. *Teaching, Research and Development.* Unpublished.

James Britton, Anthony Burgess, Nancy Martin, Alex McLeod and Harold Rosen. *The Development of Writing Abilities, 11–18.* Macmillan for Schools Council Research Series, 1975.

Bullock Report. HMSO, 1975.

A. H. Halsey. *Educational Priority,* Vol. I. p. 177. HMSO.

Nancy Martin, Pat D'Arcy, Bryan Newton and Robert Parker. *Writing and Learning Across the Curriculum 11–16.* Ward Lock for Schools Council, 1976.

Peter Medway and Ivor Goodson. "Cooperative Learning," in *Language and Learning in the Humanities.* Ward Lock for Schools Council, 1975.

Peter Medway. "How It Looks from Here," in Harold Rosen, *Language and Literacy in Our Schools.* Studies in Education, No. 1, NFER for University of London Institute of Education.

Acknowledgments

Andrew Macalpine and Dave Halligan for their second report from Thomas Calton School. The Headmaster and Staff of Westerhope Middle School for their Statement of Intent and Language Policy.

9

Tracking the Development of
Good Transactional Writing:
Some of the Problems

Since the bulk of school knowledge is transmitted through the written language in its transactional forms, reading books and writing attract increasing attention as students go up the secondary school; and most students find both difficult. In the fourth and fifth years the pressure of anxiety mounts for both students and teachers, and on the whole results in the kind of "knowledge" presented in the kind of writing quoted in the beginning of chapter three of *Writing and Learning Across the Curriculum.* We were interested in tracking, at all stages in the secondary school, the circumstances in which students make their own sense out of new information, restructure it to fit into their expanding world picture and remain at the center of their own learning. Some of our findings are reported and commented on in chapter three; there almost all examples of writing come from the eleven-to-thirteen age group. Here we indicate where our enquiry has led us in the particular circumstances of the fourth and fifth years.

We had two specific quests. First, "book knowledge," because of the importance given to it in schools. We wanted to track the circumstances in which students were able to make their own sense of this kind of secondary experience. Second, the problem of the isolated examples of good transactional writing. Could we find circumstances in which there was enough good writing in a single class, or group, for us to be able to generalize the conditions? This last has been a general aim and we think that what we have to say about the conditions for good transactional writing may in fact have a wider significance.

Most of the good transactional writing we found in the work of older

Published in *Writing and Learning Across the Curriculum 11-16*, N. Martin, P. D'Arcy, B. Newton, and R. Parker, Ward Lock Educational, 1976.

(as well as younger) students started from firsthand experience. The examples we quote here come from two groups (or classes) in the same school. The students were in their fifth year, and the writing comes from the folders of ongoing work they were collecting to present for 0 level (Mode III) social studies or CSE (Mode III) community studies. We have commented elsewhere in this book on the limiting effects of examinations on learning and writing, and have been making some case studies of written work from schools where Mode III-type examinations (assessment of course work) are taken. It is, of course, quite possible for folders of course work to be composed of set work marked in the usual way, so it is not the type of examination *per se* which causes changes. It is rather that, given a favorable environment for learning, then the writing that arises from it is the matter that is assessed for the examination. So this type of examination *permits* the kind of work normally done in the school to continue.

The firsthand experience in these course-work studies was extended, as one would hope, by secondary experience of different kinds. Different students made different use of secondary sources, some going chiefly to books for their information, others relying on what they learned from other people. Most of them draw on books and teachers for the way they organize and present their work, and in addition, they reflect on the study they have been engaged in and assess its value to them, and in doing so demonstrate some kind of perspective for their learning. At this point, therefore, we want to suggest that one of the conditions for good transactional writing is where circumstances encourage the *interplay of firsthand and secondary experience,* and that a further condition is that there should be opportunities for the students to encounter good and *varied models of transactional language.*

The term *model* here needs a word of explanation. It is not used to refer to an exemplar that is deliberately imitated. It means here the sense of what something is like, arrived at by repeated encounters. Language is learned by meeting it and using it. In chapter one we discussed how experience of living teaches us to recognize the kind of discourse that we are encountering. For instance, we seldom fail to recognize instructions when we meet them. Again we can usually identify a sales talk, even disguised as a story, or a sermon, though children can be deceived here because they are, as yet, in the process of learning the functions of these different kinds of discourse. In this sense all the examples of language use which we encounter in our daily life are models.

We found in many schools considerable poverty of varied models of transactional writing. Up to the fifth year students tended to work from a single textbook, supplemented by their teachers' notes. They just did not have enough experience of good and varied language in their different subjects.

We begin with two 0 level projects in social studies. The first, by a fifth form girl, is a very extensive project called "The Development of New Walk, Leicester." All we have space for here are quotations from her introduction and from the first half of her conclusion, but we think they indicate her purpose and the scope of her study, show something of her sources, and reveal something of the interaction between her firsthand knowledge of Leicester and the very large extent to which she has drawn on secondary sources of information. The quality of her writing reflects a wide experience of models of the written language.

The Development of New Walk

Introduction (extract)

I chose New Walk for my project because I feel it is an important part of Leicester's heritage which should be preserved. Its attractiveness led me to investigate into its past history. It fascinates me to see the old houses which stand, majestically defying the march of progress.

Another reason for my choice of project was that I wanted to learn some history without my head being crammed with dates of wars and revolutions. I learned how New Walk developed and about the life of a family who lived there. That is real history, the history of life, people and places around you which otherwise would pass by unnoticed.

I intend to research into the history of New Walk, the plans for its redevelopment, a case history of a house in New Walk, and the reasons why the Walk should be preserved.

Janet (15)

This shows her as confident in her role as a student, independent in her view of history, and she can use the language of books as her own. The two paragraphs from her conclusion which follow reveal a good deal of reading about problems of conservation, planning and development, and local information, as well as firsthand knowledge of the city. She is at ease with general ideas, and explores as well as reports problems:

After doing the project I am not so sure that this is quite what is meant by conservation. A city has been accepted as the place for work, not as a residential community, though there is a suggestion for a residential complex between High Street and Silver Street. The Council have asked for public opinion on the matter and issued two information sheets. The area is full of little quaint old shops. With rents being lower than anywhere else in the city center, one-man businesses are able to operate to make a profit. These would all be lost in any large-scale redevelopment.

We hope our city thrives on business and because of this you get a conservation of a city center which "dies" between 6 and 9 pm and 2 and 8 am. Our cities are like giant factories set in motion by the arrival of their workers and closed by their exit. In our expanding society land is becoming in very short supply. If our cities are not renovated for habitation now, we are limiting space for the people of the next generation to live. Without the conservation of places like New Walk, we are destroying the city's character to make way for prefabricated concrete office blocks that have a nine-to-five halflife.

We took Janet's study as our first example because it is so clearly the kind of work people expect in fifth form students; it is a bookish study in content and language (which is not to decry it at all).

Our second example from this fifth year 0 level group of students is by a boy. It stems from a situation in his own experience, and in one sense it is a narrative, but as his introduction shows he extends it into general questions which go beyond his own family.

Social studies project on the rehousing of my grandparents

Introduction

This project is about the rehousing of my mother's parents, Mr and Mrs J. Bird. They now live in a new set of flats, but before, they lived for thirty-five years in an old town-type house. The project will be about their views towards moving. The change of friends and community. Will it affect their way of life? Benefits of the new flat—heating etc. Criticism of the old house.

Besides answering these questions I will also try to find out how the Council go about the rehousing of individuals. How do they approach people?

Brian (15)

Then follows a narrative summary of the events in his grandparents' lives in relation to their house. We quote the last four paragraphs to illustrate the quality of his reporting and writing.

. . . this was very sad for my grandma and grandad knowing that they had to move from their own house after having bought it. I am sure they thought that it would last them the rest of their lives.

Gradually since 1972, people were leaving Vann Street, some moving into flats in Leicester and some moving outside Leicestershire altogether.

Housing Inspectors called on grandma and grandad asking them where they wanted to go. Alternative houses were offered all around Leicester, but grandma and grandad were not sure where they wanted to go.

Nearing the present day they mentioned that they were hopeful of moving into some new flats that were being built just around the corner.

Everything climaxed.

He then constructed a questionnaire for his grandparents, and this and the answers ("all answered by my grandma") are the next two items in his folder. We print the questionnaire and two of the answers:

Questionnaire for my grandparents

1. How do you feel about losing the old house and gaining a new one?
2. What benefits of a new house can you foresee?
3. How do you feel to see your old neighborhood disappearing and a change of friends, neighborhood and community?
4. How were you approached by the Council?
5. How was the "disturbance" money given out?
6. How are the flats designed?

Sample answers written by his grandmother:

1. It was very sad to know that we had got to move after buying it and having it for thirty-five years. Grandad will miss his garden at the back.
5. People who have been living in the houses for five years qualify for the "disturbance money." If you have been living in the house for five years the "disturbance money" is three times the rateable value plus twenty-five pounds for removal of furniture, cookers etc. On top of this we also got the price for the house which is £3,100.

    We shall not receive this "upheaval money" until we move into our new flat.

    On the Compulsory Purchase Order of 15th September 1972, the area was classed as unfit for human habitation. Through our estate agent we objected that we didn't live in dirt and grit. We found out that when the area was classed as unfit for human habitation it meant that not each individual house was unfit for human habitation (like ours) but that the area as a whole was classed unfit for human habitation. Later we were changed off para (a) to para (b) of the Compulsory Purchase Order thus receiving more money.

The longest item in his folder is his account of the move called "The big day." It is a lively, detailed account with vignettes of uncles and aunts and cousins who helped with the move. The family is presented, dialogue and all. His last item is a photograph from the *Leicester Mercury* with the following caption: "Derelict homes waiting for the demolition men to

move in. A distressing sight for the families who used to live in them."
Alongside this picture of ruinous houses he has written:

> After having read this my grandma nearly bit my head off for writing
> this piece with the photo. I told her I had took it from the *Mercury.*
> She answered saying that this photo was taken down one of the oldest
> streets and these are the worst condition of all the houses. She no
> doubt thought that I was implying that her house looked like this.

Then he adds in brackets, as though his grandma's reaction had made
him think again about the human implications of the photograph and the
caption:

> (Although they don't say "a typical view" in the quote, they are on
> the border to saying this.)

We have quoted a good deal from this study for several reasons. It is
very different from Janet's study which seems to us in the best academic
tradition, yet this one also is involved, independent and thoughtful work.
But while we can see in both studies the dynamic interaction of firsthand
experience and information from secondary sources, this study draws primarily on the face-to-face experience of other people, though in its organization—the introduction, the questionnaire, the arrangement of the
items—we can see the influence of books. Brian has also involved his family in his study, not only as sources of information but as active contributors, and what a model his grandma's writing is—in our view, an admirable
example of what good transactional writing should be like. His own writing draws on all his resources of speech, but it has its more formal features
too in the questionnaire and in other items which we have not the space to
include.

The outstanding feature of these studies (and of others in the group
which we have not been able to quote) is that they are genuine communications of experience of learning. They relate to the writers' own lives and
interests and reflect a sense of being on the threshold of the adult world. In
this they are realistic educational documents, and they contrast violently
both in content and language with most traditional examination answers.
We would however repeat the point made earlier: the different type of examination does not cause the change; it allows it to happen when many other conditions in the context of learning are present.

We have dealt with this question of the development of transactional
writing in the upper school at considerable length because it is the main
kind of language used in school across the curriculum. It is also the language which most troubles students—and their teachers. We have tried to
show that our evidence suggests that the way into it is not by recipe but by
the constant interaction of a personal viewpoint with information from var-

ied secondary sources. We think this dynamic is the actual process of learning as well as of language growth.

At the beginning of this chapter we discussed the problem of isolated examples of writing that showed commitment, and suggested that for such commitment to happen on a wider scale whole environments for learning would need to be changed. All the writing we have quoted in this section came from the same school but not from the same class. So these writings are not isolated examples, and we think therefore we can make the general point that for changes to go beyond the occasional individual student there must be enough teachers who share a view about learning and language to create a different set of possibilities in the school. We suggest that in this school such a different set of possibilities had been created.

IV

Next Directions:
Models, Contexts, Intentions

The significance of what children write in their stories and poems—the fables they create out of their experience—appears again as one of the themes in Part IV. Here it is seen as part of the study of contexts and intentions more generally. In the background is the counterpoint of transactional writing and its problems—the obverse of the coin to the fictive mode of dealing with experience.

10

Encounters with Models

Our children are surrounded by print from their earliest years—corn-flake packets, labels on parcels, boxes containing toys and games, grocery and frozen food packets, advertisements, birthday cards and words on the television screen, not to mention comics, magazines, newspapers and books. These are about the place—on the breakfast table, in the kitchen, by the television, on the mantelpiece, anywhere. No one tells anyone to read them; they are there for the taking. From their earliest years the children are busy sorting out the conventions and rules of use which tell them what is what in the world of print. Mostly they do this by encountering thousands of these different "models" of the printed language, so that, in the course of time, they learn from the experience of many encounters what is a story, an advertisement, or information in its many various forms. No single person teaches them this. This learning is part of the process of living in a literate society, though, of course, any person who is around may contribute to this learning *en route*, as it were. Thus, before they learn to read they have encountered printed language in many situations. Learning to read—which is specifically taught—is only the first step in learning to recognize what a particular printed item is, and thereby being in a position to interpret it.

The word *model* usually implies something to be consciously imitated, or at any rate a conscious analogy. I want to use it in the sense of an item whose use and form are recognized by repeated encounters so that we come to know, from experience, what it is we are reading.

Furthermore, I want to suggest that the processes of reading and writing are very different, one being a reception and the other a transmission

Published in *English in Education*, Vol. 10, No. 1, Spring, 1976.

process, and that while direct teaching is of primary importance in learning to read, it is possible that it should play a secondary (or consultative) role in fostering children's writing. We should, I think, rely more on the deliberate provision of many and varied models. In the transmission process which writing is, it is the writer's perception of the world, his task and the knowledge (or experience) he wishes to incorporate which is the driving force and his own language the means. The way in which language is extended is a mysterious process, part of which seems to lie in repeated encounters with models, and part in the writer's conscious or unconscious use of his own versions of these models. Consider, for example, the ratio of the words each of us has acquired by looking them up in dictionaries or being told, to those we have learned ("picked up") by just encountering them. The latter must surely account for the greater proportion. John Lyons[1] suggests that there are mutually maintained conventions and presuppositions which govern our understanding of particular types of linguistic behavior (telling a story, philosophizing, buying and selling, praying, writing a novel, etc.). If we ask how these mutually understood conventions are acquired we can only say that experience of encountering them and using them is the major part; add to this the active investigations of the learner, and much advice by others, teachers and parents for instance.

Let us look at a few of the stages in this process.

Here is Andrew, aged 3 years 11 months, investigating stories.[2]

I was entering recent happenings into the log book when Andrew came into the office. The following conversation took place:

ANDREW: What are you writing?

MISS E: Some of the interesting things that have happened here in the nursery.

ANDREW: Tell me them.

MISS E: This one says, "Mrs. Taylor and Mrs. Shotton (local inspectors) visited the nursery during the afternoon session to see the climbing frame and make arrangements for its removal."

ANDREW: What did they want to look at it for? Drew says they're going to take it away on a lorry.

MISS E: I'm hoping so. It's very rusty and dangerous for you all to use. That's why I asked Mrs. Shotton to come and see it. Then, after she had been here I wrote all about it in this book.

ANDREW: Read some more.

MISS E: "The nursery school closed for the October holidays."

ANDREW: The writing's different. Why?

MISS E: Mrs. Tindale wrote these two pages. You see, I was poorly and had to stay at home.

ANDREW: Is that in?

MISS E: Yes, here it is.

ANDREW: What are the numbers for?

MISS E: That is the date. It tells us the exact day that it happened.

ANDREW: Is it all real? Is it a true story?

MISS E: Everything in here is true. I only write down the things that actually happen.

ANDREW: Do you ever write down about the boys and girls?

MISS E: Often. Let's find some. This one tells us about the day we all went to Stanley Zoo. Here is one about Diane and the day she cut her eye and had to be taken to hospital.

ANDREW: It's a nice story book. Why have you never read it to us?

MISS E: I'm sorry that I didn't think of it. It's a lovely idea and perhaps you could even help to write it. You could let me know all the important things that happen, then I'll be sure to write them all down in this special book.

ANDREW: I bet you'll not put it with the other books though.

MISS E: No. This is a special story book so it has to stay in a special place—on my cupboard.

ANDREW: Are all books real? They're not, are they? Some of them are. The one about the farm and the car book and the sea-side, they're real. But it's hard to know. Is monkey island real? That's my favorite, except for one thing. Mrs. Stewart says the boy hasn't got a name in the book. But Zippo (the monkey) has. Do you think it's a true story?

MISS E: I'm not sure. You go and get the book and we'll see if it says so inside.

ANDREW: (returning with the book) It's not a true story. I asked in there. I don't know whether it's my favorite any more.

Andrew may or may not have met stories at home, but in the nursery he has been been read to, told stories, handled books and drawn pictures which in their way are little stories from life. In this incident he is trying to place the school log in the context of his growing experience of books. He is clearly satisfied that its contents are stories; he hasn't hitherto connected stories printed in a book with a person with a pen actually writing, so the details of the handwriting and date interest him, and this brings him to the central point of his satisfaction—"Is it all real? Is it a true story?" Then comes his judgment—"It's a nice story book. Why have you never read it to us?"—which is followed by his re-assessment of his favorite story because he discovers it is not true. At this stage he is not experienced enough in the conventions and rules of use to be sure when a story is true or when what he hears is a bit of life. He doesn't know whether to incorporate the story into his growing picture of life as it is and act upon it, so the "truth" criterion is all important. Later, when he has had more experience of stories and can recognize them easily, he will not have to be so concerned about the "is it true" issue and can enjoy them as fictions or things as they might be.

William (5 years 10 months) trying out a letter:

I had been to see William and his parents and when I left he gave me a paper albatross that he had made. The next day, when he was on his own for a time, he wrote the following letter, rushed to his mother when she came in and asked her to post it. It was unprompted and unaided. It is not at all like speech and represents his present notion of what might go into a letter—of what a letter is.

Dear Nancy I hope you and John (a friend who also knows William) will come for one small day soon give good luck to John and I give good luck to you and you and John will share that albatross and very good wishes love from William.

Clare, aged 9, wrote, unprompted and at home, the following piece of fictional natural history. It is her own version of this genre and her "knowledge" of its "conventions and presuppositions" must have come from her encounters with models of this sort and her willing representation of them *for her own purposes.*

Roski

The Roski is a cat-like animal, living in the trees. When full-grown it is black, with a sandy colored tip to its tail, and this is ringed with ginger. Its eyes are golden, and shine in the dark. Its pointed ears are edged with white. It has 4 orange claws on each foot, which help it climb. The young, or raskis as they are called are light brown marked with lighter stripes. The ears are like an adult roski. It has orange claws on its feet, 4 on the front, but only 3 on the back. Its eyes are black. When it is two years old black fur pushes up among the brown and loosens it, whereupon it gets rubbed off on the bark. It grows another claw on its hind feet, and a gold spot develops in its eye, later spreading all over it. Roskis live to about fifteen, and at 13 the eyes become paler, and at 16 they are completely white. Roskis are very hardy and can eat almost anything, but not usually meat, although one occasionally does. They always stay in one place, usually a group of tall trees in which several nests are built. They are clean animals and throw all their rubbish to the ground below. The nests are made of grass and mud, and are round. They are about 1 ft 6 ins in diameter, clean and waterproof. There are porches over the round doorways, made of mud and bark and straw.

Yvonne and Susan, in their first year at secondary school:

Yvonne and Susan[3] had been to a quarry and a museum to examine fossils. The following week they had been to the library to see what they could find about fossils in various reference books, including dictionaries and encyclopedias. Because their teacher wanted to draw together their experience of the field trip, the visit to the museum and the books they had been reading in the library, she asked them to write about fossils in the following ways:

1. a dictionary definition
2. information for an encyclopedia
3. a newspaper report
4. a poem.

Yvonne wrote:

Fossils are pieces of rock with bones of animals, and plants.

The fossil ammonite was in the Jurrassic period and is a snail like fossil with a coat of crystals (illegible) it swims along and it moves by squirting water out of the back.

"The rare fossil" (layaelay)

Yvonne—from Wreake Valley College, (Syston) has find an only fossil layaelay she is 11 years old and find it in howell quarry the fossil is 200,000,000 years old and the museum is offering 100,000 for it. The Howell quarry is now being searched for others as she has not accepted the 100,000 and the quarry it is *NOT!* open to public.

I looked at a fossil and
I did see a lovley crystals
Shining in side glittering in
the sun gleaming white
and all cracked like
an old mans face.
The outside was a
dirty colour
Creamishy browny black
little holes like moths
had eaten it I put
it back in the ground
for another person to
find

And Susan wrote:

A rock with a form of animal in it.

An Ammonite was round and has cells in it. It was a sea creature that lived in a shell.

Yesterday Susan—of Queniborough, Leics, age 11, found a rare fossil called the hypentitus it is the only one of its kind to be found, it is fifty feet in length from head to tail and ten foot wide it was the about the size of fifteen double decker buses put on top of each other.

The hypentitus is about eighty million years old. Susan said she is selling it to the Leicester Museum for ten thousand pounds, she had not decided what to do with it all yet.

The Fossil

I looked at the fossil in my hand
it was covered with golden shiny sand
and I imagined what the fossil should be.

Both girls have a pretty clear idea about what each of the four pieces of writing would be expected to contain. They are familiar enough with these kinds of writing to know that they belong to different situations and they move easily into these situations and make use of knowledge that has not been explicitly taught.

It is interesting to look at the quality of what the girls wrote. They find themselves as writers most confidently and effectively in their newspaper reports, where they feel free to improvise on the situation and surprise their imaginary readers—in reality, perhaps, an in-joke with their teacher who is an actual audience. And they are also familiar with poems and know that this means the freedom to express their personal response to the fossils in a way that draws on their everyday language—and experience—and is also free to break away as newspaper reports can't—or don't. This, more than any of the other kinds of writing they try out here, is their *own* language.

(Creamishy browny black
little holes like moths
had eaten it . . .)

The other two items, the definition and the information for the encyclopedia, are not so confidently and competently handled, although both writers have a general sense of what they "ought to be like." They know for instance that a dictionary definition is generally short, but they do not understand, or cannot cope with, the nature of the generalizations that a definition demands. Again, they know that encyclopedia items do not include a personal view, but they do not know how to select and organize the information. This is, of course, a difficult task, and depends on the writer's decision as to what selection of information his audience needs. Most children at this stage don't have enough information to select from, and Yvonne and Susan are content with a minimum; but they do know what sort of writing it should be. If books are really voices, then they can make their written pieces talk quite like encyclopedias.

What emerges from this is that children need to encounter many, many models of the written language. From these varying models they derive their notions of what writing is like and how one kind is different from another, but we all advance from the known to the less known, and perhaps in many of the specific writing tasks we set children in school we don't allow them to take their familiar language equipment with them, and they therefore fail to draw on the experience of language that they already have. By demanding (across the curriculum) too much impersonal writing addressed to an anonymous public audience (and an adult audience at that) we are perhaps stopping them from drawing on their experience of many encounters with many kinds of language, and from trying out their own versions of these. Thus, the writing task is often more like a raid into alien territory, with all its attendant risks and uncertainties, than a companionable walk through familiar country with excursions from time to time into unknown bits of the terrain.

So, children need to write about all sorts of things in all sorts of ways but some ways are easier for them than others and they need to be confident and competent in the ways of writing they feel at home in before they get too rigorous a dose of the more difficult kinds of writing. It needs emphasizing that impersonal transactional writing is more difficult for everyone, adults as well as children, because it tends to exclude a personal view and cannot therefore draw on everyday language or personal experience which are the chief means of access to thinking.

We seem to be saying that children learn to write by writing like the books they read, but while it is true that without models direct teaching would be of little use, it is also true that a teacher has a crucial role as an instigator of writing, a provider of models and a reader of what the children write. How much there is available to read in children's lives outside school varies enormously, so the importance of school as a place where models abound is great. And this means, of course, time to read, to talk about books, books (i.e. print) about the place, writings on the walls—in short, a reading climate.

This raises the question of which models are most important. The answer here is given in the four pieces by Yvonne and Susan—those models are most important which children *can make use of* because they have something in common with the language and viewpoint of children; and this means, more than anything else, literature—stories, poems, plays—which is structured on a personal viewpoint. James Britton, in the first teacher's book accompanying the *Oxford Books of Stories for Juniors,* observes the "stories and poems will have more in common with children's speaking and writing than will any other forms of written language in use in school" because both are forms of "personal language." He says, "it is as much as most children can do to see the world, and describe it from their own individual point of view." They may begin to have an inkling of how it looks to their mothers, or sisters, or a pet, but that is a long way from seeing things in general from the point of view of people in general, i.e. the impersonal viewpoint.

Fortunately stories and poems abound in most schools, but opportunities for children to encounter good transactional writing are more limited, especially in secondary schools where a variety of models is not usually part of the picture of subject teaching. Here the available models are often limited to a single textbook for a year and the teacher's explanations and notes—and sometimes worksheets, which tend to be like textbooks. Yvonne and Susan were fortunate in that their work on fossils included field study, museum study, work in the library and opportunities to assimilate their knowledge by writing about it in various ways. Such range is relatively rare across the curriculum as a whole. This may be partly due to a failure to recognize the role of wide experience of other people's language as well as a wide range of opportunities for the writer; and it may be partly due to the fact that good transactional writings are hard to come by. People are not so concerned about the quality of informational writing. They seem to gauge it in different ways from literature. Is the information accurate, for instance, or is it up to date, or is it an appropriate selection, or presented in a way that is easy to memorize? All of these are indeed important, but the quality of writing is more significant than is perhaps realized, since so much of language development seems to be a matter of *indirectly* acquiring the voice—or more hopefully the voices—of the available models.

Outside school thousands of models in informational writing crowd at us from printed instructions, guide books, technical magazine articles, advertisements etc., where the criterion is concerned with the ability to cram the most information into the least space, and where there is no feedback from the audience. So teachers who could search out powerful informational writing to be available as indirect models for the children who read them would be breaking new ground.

To conclude with a true story which readers must interpret as they will:

There was a class in a Midland Junior School where the work as reflected in what the children wrote in their exercise books was mechanical, scrappy and badly done. In some of the children's books, as well as the tasks set, there were a number of pieces copied out, probably from textbooks. All were brief bits and pieces except one, and this one copied piece stood out by the fact that the boy kept it up during three days, copying it before and after the interruptions that his set work seemed to constitute. The handwriting of this piece (alone) was beautiful, and it occupied five full pages—much the greatest amount that anyone wrote. It was the only language of imagination or quality that could be found in the books of this class. Here is part of it.

Wasps

The Buzzing can be heard in gardens and field in summer time and autumn. The wasps are looking for nectar in the flowers. They settle on fruit in the orchards and suck the sweet juice. Bees may be flying there too. The wasps are a brighter yellow and smoother than the bees. The wasp has two very large eyes. On her head also are two long black feelers. With these she can smell and feel her way about. Only the queen lives through the cold winter. She sleeps or hibernates in a sheltered place. It may be the bark of a tree or under some dry leaves. On a warm day in spring the queen wasp wakes. She crawls out into the sunshine and spreads her wings. She feeds on nectar from the flowers. Then she looks round for somewhere to build a new nest. The queen wasp may find a hole left by a field mouse or a mole . . .

Notes and References

1 John Lyons. *Structural Semantics,* Blackwell, 1964.
2 With acknowledgments to Sarah Evans, of Newton Hall Nursery, Framlingate Moor, Co. Durham.
3 With acknowledgments to Pamela Lunn at Wreake Valley College—and to Yvonne and Susan.

11

Scope for Intentions:

Contexts for Writing with Special Reference to Unassessed Journals Written for the Teacher

This paper has a dual focus; one is on the contexts for writing, the other on the significance of self-directed writing in the development of general writing ability.

Work over five years with the British Schools Council Project, *Writing across the Curriculum 11 to 16 years,* had suggested that the development of writing ability might be as much a product of the school contexts as of the quality of the teaching or the ability of the students. (Martin et al. 1976) We observed that where we found good writing in any quantity *in any one class* it seemed to be related to scope for intentions, using the term with the meaning that Bruner gives it in his work with infants as a gatherer of tacit powers. (Bruner 1975) Scope for intentions in turn seemed to be related to particular features in the learning environment—to the contexts of the school, and in particular to the reciprocity of intentions of the teachers and students. Consequently, when working in Western Australia in 1978 on a survey of English in the Government High Schools, we set out to study particularly the contexts for English to attempt to identify the constraints and liberating features for students and teachers and to see how the intentions of each fared in different circumstances. We supposed that we should find groups of interacting influences, not single ones.

At one end of the scale we tried to tap the quality of what went on in classrooms. We assumed that understandings, beliefs and values are major determinants of the environments that people create. At the other end we studied the effect of what Parlett and Hamilton (1976) call the "manage-

First published in *Learning to Write: First Language, Second Language,* A. Freedman, I. Pringle, and J. Yalden (eds.). Longman, 1983.

ment framework"—the arrangements belonging to the organization of the school and its place in the system; such things as assessment procedures, time-tabling, length of lessons, room changing, copying facilities, etc., all of which can powerfully influence the life of classrooms. Between these two contextual dimensions is the English department and the senior English teacher. Here, hierarchy may or may not be powerful; consultation may or may not take place; decisions may or may not be shared. Working on what we thought we knew about the possibilities arising from groups of teachers with shared intentions, we looked specially at the way English departments worked as influential features in the contexts for writing.

This paper is based on a case study of one school. (Martin et al. 1980) Here it reports only on the written work, which is set throughout in its context of the beliefs and attitudes and ways of working of the group of teachers who constituted the English department. Our aim was to document all that could be observed about the effect of reciprocity of intentions on the development of writing.

The School Context

We chose this particular school because the senior English master had been funded by the Schools Commission (Federal Funding Agency) to develop talk and personal writing as a means of learning in all subjects. An additional reason was that he and the other English teachers believed that students should understand and participate in the aims of the department—or in the case of younger students understand why they were asked to do this or that. To achieve this, students needed to reflect, in talk or writing, on their own learning. The forms of writing that offer most scope for reflection are journals, and in an alternative mode, poems and stories. To this end, the keeping of personal journals written for the teacher, but unassessed, were made part of the regular program in the upper school, and imaginative writing was also a permanent option.

We looked only at the work of two classes, years 11 and 12. We chose upper-school classes because that is where examination pressure is greatest and the scope for writing most likely to be restricted; and we chose to look at English rather than English Literature because English is a compulsory subject in the Tertiary Admissions Examination and therefore the range of student ability is relatively wide. We were interested in the effects of the contexts for writing on the *general* level of writing rather than in exceptional pieces by a few committed students.

Mutual Understanding and Intent:
Some Illustrations

Year 12 students were asked to discuss in small groups what they thought were the aims of upper-school English, and then to write individual statements. One student in a typical statement wrote:

> I think the first and foremost aim is to ensure we all pass the Trumpet (TAE). I know the teachers try to convince us and themselves that this isn't the main aim but when it all boils down, the only reason we are at school is to receive our TAE certificate.
>
> I think other than this the teachers aim to:
>
> * allow us to be able to formulate our own ideas and express them with confidence within a group.
> * give us a wide diversity of reading so that we can learn to appreciate all kinds of literature.
> * help us develop our sense of creativity and learn the joys of writing things for ourselves.
> * let us develop our own unique style of expression.

Another wrote:

> Certainly English is a curriculum where a student can learn about himself.... The English lessons should also be enjoyable, an oasis from the rest of school drudgery. Unlike other subjects, English is an avenue for developing and putting to use creativity and imagination.

Perhaps the most surprising thing about these statements is that "passing the Trumpet" is seen as distinct from all other aims. The students did not see them as connected in any way. Yet, if the first writer's aim were fulfilled, the students would pass their examinations in their stride, which they apparently do. Subsequently the students were given the printed aims of the English department and were surprised to find it so similar to their own much-valued independent views. The whole exercise was a step towards mutual understanding.

Part of the management framework of a big school, or department, is the circulation of written notices. If we look at some of the printed documents that the senior English master got out from time to time, we can see that he worked with the staff—as with the students—by a process of explanation, consultation and discussion. His circulars were for information *and* discussion; some were just for discussion. They were brief, and the sense of orders coming from above was counteracted by their personal tone, and sometimes an eccentric heading, for example: "How I learnt to stop worrying, love the English department and let it run itself: some notes on administration." Others appear to take up an ongoing conversation as in a circular for discussion by the staff about the assessment of written work where he wrote:

> I explained to my class that I believed they wrote best when they wrote for a real purpose and a real audience . . . and that they would learn to write by writing. I suggested that as I believed assessment could affect the quality of their work negatively, I would only assess five pieces of work during the term. My original intention was to tell them which five pieces of work would be assessed. They asked instead that they hand up what they thought were their five best pieces, and I agreed . . . .

He took parents into his confidence in a similar way; explained to them and asked for their help. In a circular about homework he wrote:

> We believe that students learn to write by writing—perhaps in much the same way that they learn to talk by talking. . . .
>
> Although the benefits of reading, writing and talking are not always obvious, we believe that these do contribute significantly to students' development . . . .
>
> Many parents may enjoy reading the novels which their children read as part of the English course. Often these novels deal with issues of significance to adolescents, and reading with your children may lead to interesting and worthwhile conversations with them.

And again in his sheet for students he introduced the assignments by explaining as well as giving instructions, thus:

> I believe the best assignments are those that evolve as a result of reading combined with the personal experience of the writer. So you are asked to do some background reading. This may be either fiction or non-fiction; you could also include the viewing of television films or listening to the radio as part of this background work.
>
> It is expected that you become involved in a personal way in the assignment. Try interviews—but don't just report what was said; describe your reaction to what was said . . . if you're writing about primary education, visit one or two schools, interview some teachers and some children.

About journals he wrote:

> It should consist of your own personal expressive writing. You may write in any form you like, or a variety of forms including poetry, prose, drama or art work. Write about things that are important to you. It can be written, if you like, for a private, restricted audience . . . it should show your view of life and of the world in which you live.

There are a number of other documents which space does not allow me to quote, but they all carry significant implicit messages. They assert a belief in relationships based on face-to-face talk irrespective of status within the school hierarchy; and this goes for students as well as staff. As a result the English staff have created an environment in which reading and writing and the discussion of ideas is part of the life of the department staff and students alike. The staff room is itself a continuing seminar for ideas about literature, about writing, about education, and about the place of language in learning.

The Writing Program

Writing in Subject English: Two Directions or One?

The program for writing seemed to fall into two parts—the development of general writing ability, and specific preparation for the TAE examination. Each was treated with similar thoroughness and understanding of its value to students. It is often assumed that these two directions are mutually exclusive. The work in this school demonstrated that they are not. The preparation for the TAE paper is dealt with cursorily here because it is very much what all teachers do, whereas the development of general writing ability, and, by implication, the development of intellect and personality, is not something that all teachers concern themselves with.

In a circular to the English staff the senior English master dealt with all the practical and administrative matters of the written English exam—information about the availability of test material and past papers, warnings that concentration on test material is not the best way to help students pass their exams, advice about the need to put some pressure on—and also the need to take it off—and a reminder that literature is always at the back of good writing. It was all there, and the implications and problems and decisions were taken up in discussions in the English staff room, and in class with the students.

Assignments and Options

Students in year 11 undertake one long assignment; in year 12 they do two. An assignment may take from six weeks to a term or more to complete. The English teachers regard these long-term assignments as of major importance both for students' general development and for their writing. Options in both years regularly include a six weeks journal, any topic of their own choosing or a major "creative work"—a play, radio play, a set of poems, or two or more short stories. In addition, optional topics are suggested by the teachers. In 1978 these were Unemployment, Your Future Career, Old Age, Immigration, Primary or Special Education.

About the suggested topics one might be tempted to think that they are limited by their sociological slant, but the emphasis that these teachers place on firsthand experience needs remembering; this itself places a limit on the topics. Furthermore, in every assignment, one of the options is "a topic of your own choosing." This, together with the option to write stories, poems or plays, gives scope for more imaginative directions. And there is the journal.

That all these are long assignments perhaps needs some elaboration. The process of writing an extended piece of work is radically different from even a self-chosen essay. First, there is the fact that a long assignment includes a whole variety of self directions—the topic, the background reading, individual sources of information, mode of treatment, variety of language forms, etc. Second, there is the "progressive refocussing" or the changes of direction made possible by the time span and the gradual penetration of the field of study. Third, the time span allows for unconscious processes to get to work so that a sense of the whole operation can begin to inform and shape the parts. Finally, since diary entries are a recommended part of the work, there is a built-in focus on reflection both on the field of study itself, and on the learning process intrinsic to the study. Throughout, the writer is able to make choices so his intentions are at a premium. It is clear that all the options give scope for the students' own directions, and what is singular about the topics suggested by the teachers is that they comprise only those where firsthand experience is possible. (The role of firsthand experience in learning is discussed in the next section.)

Thus, the connection between the perceptible form of the writing curriculum and the learning priorities of the teachers is clear. They know what they are doing and why. We thought this was a contextual feature of importance and discuss it more fully later.

Language as an Educator: Discussion of the Theory Behind the Writing Program

The writing program with its extensive options is not random, nor merely a collection of stimulating suggestions. It expresses the *conscious* operating constructs of the teachers in the English department about the nature of writing and its relation to learning. The following discussion is based on conversations with staff and students and on reading most of what the students had written.

Scope for Intentions: Commitment

Intention is a difficult word to use in so broad a context. It is used here to cover a wide spectrum. At one end are those concerns which cause students to write this rather than that in free choice situations—which concerns are often unrecognized until expressed; and on the part of teachers, the fostering of students' attempts to find their own directions in the belief that this is how powers of language and thought are most easily gathered. At the other end are all the manifold deliberate intentions such as practicing comprehension tests for the exam, or writing a journal three times a week, or any other decision to do this or that. We were interested in the significance of intention as an aspect of commitment to writing and to learning. It is this aspect that is the special concern of this paper.

As it operated in the teaching and learning of English in this school, commitment appeared to consist of a commitment to a relationship, and a commitment to learning.

Commitment to a Relationship

The commitment to a relationship seemed to work in both a general and a specific way. In the general way, students and teachers knew what they were doing and why. There was a transparent rationality about the whole operation of writing which made it entirely possible for students to make sense of their place in it and identify with its purposes. (See their account of the aims of the English department.) Their assent was given on the basis of full information; they had access to principles and rationale.

In the specific way, the writings carry a sense of a private line to the reader (the teacher usually), always important in genuine communication. The extracts from the journals which follow convey a sense of writing for an audience known to be attentive, appreciative, sensitive and humorous— an audience adequate to the *range* of moods and perceptions the writers want to express. These teachers were not only democratic and rational; they were also friends. There is a solidarity assumed between them and the writers so that together they can laugh at the establishment figures (the doctor) or contemplate the misfortunes of the original Anzac.

Commitment to Learning: Firsthand Experience and Secondary Sources of Information

The crucial aspects of intention (as affecting the strength of the writing as a process of intellectual transformation of knowledge or experience) seem to be:

1. the intention to understand P—to get it clear, put it in order, display its sections, for oneself.
2. the intention to communicate it to Q—to tell Q about it; Q being (in school) a particular person, or some idea of an ideal reader—probably a mixture of the two.

Much work in English is centered on experience, real (the writer's) or imagined (literature), but students have also to learn to write in non-literary forms and this involves the mastery of secondary experience—information and "book knowledge." It is this latter which almost invariably gives the greatest difficulties to students and teachers. Transactional writing for a particular reader would help, but the socially desired form is for a public audience, and students are not usually in a position to write authoritatively for a public audience on informational topics; hence the dilemma. First-hand experience, however, can be the means by which students can enter and make sense of secondary experience. It gives authority because its references are in external reality. (Polanyi 1969) It is for this reason that only those (informational) topics which can be rooted in firsthand experience are suggested as options. Furthermore, the kinds of writing which most directly reflect firsthand experience—journal entries, direct observation and sustained reflective commentary—are asked for as part of the presentation if the informational assignment is chosen. That all the assignments require some writing in the spectator role is an expression of the teachers' belief that knowledge is personal and, in young writers particularly, needs to be explored in personal language before it can be adequately presented more formally for a public audience.

Literature

It is when books relate to our own experience that we can immediately sense their power. This is particularly true of literature. We find that things we had assumed to be ineffable can be articulated and the possibilities of experience explored in imagination (and writing), whether in terms of Walter Benjamin's prototype of the storyteller from the locality who recounts the familiar, or the seafarer from afar with his tales of the extraordinary (Benjamin 1973). Few of the students were *explicit* about the relationship between literature and their experience, but their *tacit* understanding was expressed in the fact that the majority took up the option of "creative writing." A feature of this was the students' interest in the process and stages of their writing. Most included observations about occasions and emotions from which the work seemed to have originated together with comments about their intentions and the extent to which they were satisfied. This was not requested; it seemed to be an outcome of taking it for granted that their teachers would be interested in whatever interested the writers. It seemed that the unrestricted scope offered by the journals— once perceived and used—led the students to move into other modes, particularly poetry or narrative; and to find that the *forms* of these gave them a different kind of scope.

Some Examples from the Journals

Many of the students commented on the way things had gone for them:

STUDENT A. Because I was so apprehensive and inhibited my first few pieces were very blunt and somewhat similar to a history book . . .

reading back over what I've written, my change from formal impersonal English to a flowing and natural style is evident, and by ambigu-
ous, self-critical and half conversational types of writing I amused
myself making the hassel of writing every night pleasurable ... The
most outstanding value gained for me was that I became more aware
of the outside world ...

STUDENT B. I found that with writing regularly, my ability to write improved enormously, not only in the quality of the result but in the
ease of actually doing the writing ... I often used my writing as a
thought formulating process ...

The journal also helped me to understand myself and my place in
life.... In a very direct way this better understanding of myself
helped me to develop an identity and gain confidence in myself as an
individual ... I wrote what I really thought and felt—what I wanted
to write, and what was "me."

STUDENT C. When I started writing it (the journal) I hoped to make my
journal more interesting by making it more for public consumption. I
suppose I am a person who likes other people knowing what I think
about things ... I am quite happy to show my journal around, because clarifying things for myself, I feel it quite a challenge to write
something which people comment on ...

STUDENT D. I know that I can improve my writing by writing something
which only you (teacher) and myself can read. I dislike others reading
what I write because I fear that they may think it dribble (so to
speak). To tell you the truth I have lost some of my inhibitions as the
year goes on through writing a journal at home ...

In reading the journals (with permission) one notices both their diversity and some similarity. Perhaps the similarities are aspects of adoles-
cence and of their shared school lives, but the diversities are more startling.
Many include poems; some take on a persona—and a style to match—and
obviously enjoy the game; others present a whole range of experimental
forms and lay-outs; even the least able write direct and thoughtful pieces.

STUDENT E. (This journal is characterized by the way the writer uses language in any way he wants, and obviously enjoys doing so. It is much
taken up with observations about his work, about breaking his leg,
and about poetry.)

I think I went fairly well (in a maths exam) after such a disastrous
start, and this is probably because I enjoy maths so much this year.
You would too if you had Captain Brown for a teacher. With a
unique combination of nautical terminology and mathematical theory
delivered at great volume through the smoke haze of the occasional
Marlborough, one cannot help but pay attention ...

(After breaking his leg) It is my considered opinion that old Davies (doctor) is at the center of a sordid little conspiracy to rip off the ignorant and unhealthy of this town ... The old Gremlin was hunched over a pile of papers, writing furiously. He was unimpressed by the drama which surrounded my entry ...

I havn't been so goddam bored as this ever, even. I can't go to school because I can't walk without crutches ... Chronic boredom like this calls for desperate remedies, and I now resort to poetry writing, whether you like it or not ... (Unlike some of his other poems, this is a mocking one).

(An incident from the Anzac Day Parade) The parade was long since over and the accompanying festivities were drawing to a close. A hundred yards from the door of a rusting iron roofed hovel, an old man had managed to prop himself into a sitting position against a nearby lamp post. The bottle from which he had been drinking rolled from infirm hands ... A row of medals pinned in random precision to the lapel of his suit was mute testimony to his part in the dawn parade. He was an original Anzac ...

(The story concludes)... The men in the white car who came to take him away seemed to agree that he had asphyxiated in his own vomit ... I thought it strange that a man who had braved so much and been a distinguished soldier should have suffered the indignity of being slain by such an enemy.

STUDENT F. (Two items only from an extremely varied and well-presented collection.) Address Unknown (The opening of a longish piece)

Where I am now is through no influence of my own. An old man made me and an old lady helped. Old, that is, in relation to my youngness. They have been there. Not only by them was I made. I was made through circumstances, instances, feelings, moods, times, places: by people. I was made by impression because I am an impressionable person. I was created by a stranger whom I met on the wharf, and a foreign lady with a very strong will. Indeed, not solely by my parents. ...

Our Kitchen Table

Many years it has withstood bangings, cuttings, jolting and
    cluttering
Long has it stood unheeded, quiet, unobtrusive
Now in the corner, now along the wall
I remember Mama making scones on it at shearing time
And how Janice (who came to help) spilt some water ...
And nearly electrocuted herself ...
It was still there when we came back after two years.
Ruth made bread on that table, and afterwards

We all sat round and ate it hot.
I have often sat there, head in my arms, bewildered,
Or, talking over a cup of tea with Barb.
Plain table top, smooth with age, at each leg a convenient toe hold
And under each leg a folded piece of paper
For balance you know.

STUDENT G. (Written more at the level of daydream than reflection but
the entries capture the ebb and flow of feeling.)

Since sitting here, (for ten minutes) many strange thoughts have
come over me; this is the first time I have deliberately sat and thought
back over the days, people I have known, experiences, and what's in
store ... I'm just filling in a few minutes before Paul comes ... I
havn't been out for so long and I just love going out ... I'm getting
nervous about what I'm going to talk about ... I havn't done anything exciting ...

I'm just loving this exploring and research topic in Geography (a
field study) so much that I intend to write to the Career Center to see
if they can advise me on a career that is based on such work. I might
ask about archeology ... I think I might join the Historical Society
also ...

It's good being sick, lazing in bed, radio, drinks, and imagination
going wild ... One minute I want to go on the dole, travel the beach-
es and rage continuously—then next I want to be a teacher, have a
nice flat, a dog and live a conservative, simple life like the rest of us
... I'm sure people in this world don't do what they want to do, but
just what others would like them to ...

I have some exciting news—Donna and I came second in the State
wide open Geography competition; that was for our assignment (field
study). It's great to know that all that hard work is rewarded—50.00.
I feel rather proud actually and it's the first time I have ever won a
prize at anything.

Doubts are sometimes expressed as to whether experience of the kind
of writing quoted above from Student G is a factor in learning to use the
more formal and impersonal modes. That this student and her partner won
a prize for a Geography field study suggests that these writing skills and the
consciousness of process that goes with them do become part of a wider
writing process. Evidence from the exam results of all these students sup-
ports this view. How the English teachers viewed this is expressed in what
two of them said in written statements:

MRS. K. Perhaps the journal could be said to combine the best of both
worlds, speaking and writing. They speak to their journals certainly,
in a different, more cultivated language than that of spoken conversa-

tion, but infinitely more expressive than the kind of writing on which so much emphasis is placed in many classrooms.

MR. G. Writing in this sustained, informal kind "frees the hand." Rather than fighting every word, willing it on to the page, it gradually becomes a fully natural response, i.e. the writer is not alienated from his writing. This allows the full subject to come to expression . . . he has a larger reserve of experience to draw on which is available to him now, in the sense that many of the negative censorships operating on his discourse are now qualified and diminished.

It enables the student to observe himself and hence to develop a more objective sense of himself as a social being, at once a person for himself and for others.

In conclusion I want to suggest that school writing generally gives few opportunities for students to reflect about their own learning, to think about thinking, and to begin to know themselves. Journals offer such opportunities and the ones studied are convincing evidence of their value. But this is not the whole of the story. Writing which expresses the movements of the mind (instead of dissembling), as Peter Medway says, is a transaction which takes place between people who experience themselves as autonomous and mutually respecting parties—equals at least in the right to speak and be heard, if not in knowledge or wisdom. The journals written in this school (and the other writings) were effective as genuine communications in the context of English in this school; they came about in its climate of talk and mutuality of intentions. In less favorable circumstances where the contexts for English were different and where they might be set as just another type of written exercise, they would be unlikely to be effective in the development of writing ability and the movements of the mind that go with it.

References

Walter Benjamin. "The Storyteller," in *Illuminations.* Fontana, 1973.

Jerome Bruner. "The Ontogenesis of the Speech Act," in *Child Language,* 1975.

Nancy Martin, Pat D'Arcy, Bryan Newton and Robert Parker. *Writing and Learning Across the Curriculum 11–16.* Ward Lock, 1976.

Nancy Martin, Marnie O'Neill and Philip Deschamp. *What Goes On in English Lessons: Case Studies from Government High Schools in Western Australia.* Education Department, Western Australia, 1980.

M. Parlett and D. Hamilton. "Evaluation as Illumination," in *Curriculum Evaluation Today: Trends and Implications.* (ed) D. Tawney, Macmillan Research Series, 1976.

Michael Polanyi. *Knowing and Being.* University of Chicago Press.

12

Contexts Are
More Important
Than We Know

Perhaps the contexts for learning are more important than we know. Most people see successful teaching in terms of individual teachers. If they speak of a school as good they usually mean it has a lot of good teachers. Time was when we thought teams of inspectors, or superintendents, could go into lessons and assess what was going on as good or less good. In the 1980s this must be regarded as simplistic. Not only have our notions of the nature and role of evaluation changed, but our belief in the independence of teaching and learning from their contexts is changing too. We are now much more aware of all those elements in the school environment which affect teaching and know that we discount them at our peril. Good teachers are less willing to go on regardless, and are beginning either to move out of the profession, or to abandon the kinds of teaching dictated by their skill and imagination. Lessons are only part of the picture. Evaluators need also to identify those features of the school context which support or inhibit the work that teachers are trying to do. An analysis is needed of the whole environment for learning which a given school provides, and how the various elements in this context affect what goes on in lessons.

In this paper, *context* is taken to mean all that surrounds classroom events including the beliefs and attitudes of the teacher, the way the participants in the lesson see the classroom events, together with those aspects of the school context which impinge on the teacher's intentions; in short, the whole environment for teaching and learning.

First published in *Timely Voices: English Teaching in the 1980's*, R. Arnold (ed.), Melbourne, Oxford University Press, 1983.

No One in the Classroom Is Neutral

So we have a classroom with a lesson going on, some students, a teacher, and a visitor. The visitor may have come to assess the lesson or just to learn what is going on, but few would now dispute that the observer is part of what he observes. The meanings that each person gives to events relate to his past experience—to the systems of beliefs and attitudes arising from his life history; i.e. we each construe events through our own dark glasses, though, if we grow up within a common culture, many events may look much the same to us. Furthermore, whether the observer has an official assessment to make or not, he or she will be evaluating events for himself—checking what is going on against his own experience and trying to see where they lead. He is, in fact, relating local events in, say, an English lesson, to his wider system of beliefs about learning and education. And, of course, this is also true for all the participants in the lesson. Thus, behind the classroom events there is the interaction of all the motivational forces springing from these networks of individual self-systems. And, of course, the fact that our notions of objectivity are changing does not mean that an observer's suggestions may not be valuable. We all need listeners, and a good listener can ask questions—real questions—which prompt us to tell the story of what we are doing in a lesson and why. This articulation helps us to uncover behavior and purposes which we may not have been aware of. Then subsequent suggestions are freed to be acted on.

The different ways in which people perceive the same or similar events is illustrated by the following excerpts from a sample survey[1] of how participants and parents perceived Subject English.

A 12-year-old student said:

English is to get better at what you already know about the language.

A 13-year-old said:

English is to make us more interesting people.

Another 13-year-old said:

You learn about poetry and Shakespeare for the kids in the future. You might not like to learn about them, but the kids in the future might like to.

A 17-year-old said:

To me English is an art. Nobody can really tell you how to write. We have to go our own way now.

A parent said:

> English is a subject in their school work, isn't it? Or is it the way they
> are speaking?

Teachers' views showed a similar diversity.

Beyond Surface Curriculum: Personal Constructs

The term *personal construct*[2] has been used to refer to the systems of
beliefs and attitudes which underlie behavior, and are the unseen prompters—perhaps *determiners* is not too strong a term—of action. And these
same prompters are the major influence on each teacher's classroom climate for learning rather than those surface features of the curriculum—
books, resources, programs, etc.: beliefs about children and how they learn;
about authority and the teacher's role in the learning process; about himself
or herself as a person as well as a teacher and how both roles can be maintained within the structure of the institution which school is. In addition
there are the teacher's beliefs about Subject English; his or her views about
what English is; what the terms *language* and *literature* represent in classroom events; how children learn to progress in reading, writing and understanding books. These, together with overriding beliefs about education
and one's place in it, are likely to be the most powerful elements in the context of one's lessons.

Other Contextual Features Affecting Lessons: the Managerial System[3]

Many elements in school life impinge on what goes on in classrooms.
A teacher may or may not be able to carry out the work he wants to do
because of what has been called "the managerial system" of the school. The
term refers to those features of school life which are concerned with ongoing arrangements for the continuity and coordination of all the diverse activities. It includes such things as time-tabling, allocation of rooms,
movements about the building, extent of set programs, work assessments,
departmental allowances and departmental rooms, availability of books, use
of the library, out-of-school visits, messages from the school administration
and the way they are transmitted (or fail to be transmitted), the availability
of staff to be talked to by students, the measure of student responsibility—
the list goes on and on, and one begins to perceive its effect on what goes
on in classrooms as one enumerates items not always perceived as having
anything to do with classroom learning.

It also becomes clear that these managerial aspects of context are partly products of the whole educational system, and partly products of individual schools. The latter would seem to arise from the beliefs and attitudes of

the principal and senior staff and must be held to account for a large part of
the differences between schools, which after all operate to a broadly common curriculum and examination system and might, on the face of it, be
thought to be very similar places. Yet, if one probes beyond these common
surface features one finds very different things going on in English classrooms, and many different levels of learning occurring. How are these differences to be accounted for? And what is to be learned from
understanding them?

I want to suggest that the differences can chiefly be traced to two
sources: a teacher's personal constructs, and the extent to which the managerial system in his school allows him to teach according to these. The relationship is a complex one inasmuch as there are so many individual and
collective directions to be accommodated; but were the relationship properly understood, its effects on teaching and learning could be less random,
and the contextual features could be designed to promote the quality of
classroom experience. The difficulty is that we are talking not so much
about behavior as about the springs of behavior, and we have as yet few
tools of enquiry for arriving at what these really are, and how they change.
If a teacher's beliefs and feelings are indeed the prime movers in creating
the quality of classroom experience, then these prompters of action and
judgment need to be made explicit and open to modification through talk
with others. This would carry implications for a focus on mutual communication within a school, and for the responsibility of the managerial system
to legislate for it.

Penetrating the Quality of Classroom Experience

The authors of an illuminating study[4] of teachers' understandings of
events in their classrooms suggest that we need a paradigm for research
which would be as much concerned "with the quality of experience and the
meaning of behavior as with the occurrence of behavior"—a shot across the
bows at much current educational research—and they suggest a number of
strategies "aimed at eliciting meaning and uncovering various qualities of
experience, thought and production." In the report of their study, and in a
subsequent survey of English in Government High Schools in Western
Australia, the following strategies were the chief tools of enquiry, an enquiry which attempted to penetrate beyond surface curriculum, and in the case
of the survey, to account for the relation of contextual features to successful
and less successful English lessons:

- Structured in-depth interviews with English teachers willing to explore their work with an interviewer-discussant.
- The documentation of learning environments, especially lessons, and
open discussion with participants of how each perceived the lessons.

- Analysis of work products.
- Documentation of how students, parents, and teachers perceived the teaching and learning of English.

Space will not allow a full account of what these studies threw up. They are fully described and discussed in the two reports referred to above.

The In-depth Interview

The in-depth, structured interview together with observation and discussion of particular lessons proved the most effective way of drawing out the beliefs which seemed to underlie the classroom behaviors which the teachers valued most, yet interviews have special problems, one of which is what status to give the statements made. Even an open and relaxed interview carries its own context, and there is inevitably a gap between the statements and the events observed in the classroom. People say what they intend, or hope, should happen, aspiration being a vital aspect of teaching; but the social context of the interview works to cause them to say what they think may be socially or educationally acceptable.

In order to neutralize the social context of the interview, we began by asking what teachers had done in a recent lesson that they would like to describe. Given this option, most teachers moved into what was near their hearts, and almost all then qualified their accounts by reasons. Thus the gap between stated intentions and classroom events was narrowed by locating the statements in the context of actual lessons. The questions about recent classroom events were followed by others of a practical kind derived from issues in the educational scene: the effect of class size, use of groups, arrangements of desks, mixed ability classes, the place of literature, the value of exercises, for example. Discussion of these matters—always in the context of their own lessons—led in turn to a consideration of features in the life of their own schools which impinged, negatively or positively, on the aspects of their work they valued most. If the teachers failed to qualify the stories of their lessons by some reference to general ideas, it was easy for the interviewer to probe for these. What emerged from these interviews (one- to one-and-a-half hours) was a tissue of practicalities embedded in the contexts of the teachers' educational beliefs.

We thought these interviews yielded two different kinds of information. On the one hand, there was the picture of the scope of ongoing activities and of the nature of the students' encounters with books, drama, projects, exercises, etc., where at one extreme teachers kept close to provided resources, and at the other extreme tried to develop their own materials and used them in many different ways; on the other hand, there were the organizing ideas—or learning priorities—which, we thought, lay behind these variations in classroom practice. A study of these interview-discussions enabled us to see that some teachers put more emphasis on what might be called cognitive aspects of the work, and others on personal and social development. Overall, some priorities reflected broad developmental concerns and others rather narrow, conventional concerns. What seemed to distinguish the various learning priorities was their measure of comprehensiveness. For instance, some teachers were content if they themselves could distinguish students' progress in language skills, while others were also concerned that students should be aware of the purposes of their work, should reflect on their learning, and should inject their own intentions into the classroom activity.

Other Tools of Enquiry

We looked at our analyses of these interview-discussions alongside transcripts of our interviews with students who had participated in the lessons and found that the variations in the ways students perceived their classroom activities seemed to correspond to the learning priorities of the teachers. For instance, students in some classes took part in what was going on for better or for worse, liked some things and disliked others, and judged what they did primarily by this criterion. Other students in different classes reflected on their learning experiences in a much broader way. Apart from individual rebels and thinkers, an understanding of the educational directions of their work was mostly present among students taught by teachers with comprehensive learning priorities. Compare, for instance, familiar comments by students about which parts of English are boring or interesting with the following conversation between three 12-year-old students and an interviewer in a school where the English staff discuss their work a great deal amongst themselves and with their students.

BEVAN: I find it easier to talk on, write and explain things that I know about and have experienced and have heard about or read than something you are making up out of your own mind and you don't know anything about.

INTERVIEWER: If we've each only done a certain number of things, where would the new things come from?

DAVID: I think it's when you read books you find out things . . . different things . . . Well, visiting different places, speaking to different people, you find out different things.

INTERVIEWER: Are you thinking about excursions—or drama?

DAVID: Yeh, it makes you aware that you've got to . . . It's not always things in the classroom . . . We do a lot of work and then Mrs. S. knows when we are getting worn out and takes us outside—for drama like that—for a couple of days.

PETER: That's more or less, um, Mrs. S. She is trying to teach us . . . This is how I think that, um, English is more . . . of a way of life. That it's not just bookwork and studying a lot.

Here we have not only the children's perceptions about English lessons, but their awareness of their teacher's purposes for them.

Our third source of enquiry, the observation of lessons and the subsequent discussion of what we had observed, reinforced what we had derived from the interviews, and also revealed the pressures from the managerial system. The three sets of data gave us some evidence for our hypotheses about the underlying forces in the classroom, and the effects of external arrangements upon these. Outstanding in what emerged from our interviews was the teachers' desire for freedom to teach as they thought best, and different teachers identified different features in the context of the school as preventing or assisting their work. It seemed that those with the most comprehensive learning priorities suffered most. For example, prescribed programs of set texts, chapter by chapter, linked to weekly assessments, made long assignments, *ad hoc* events, drama and projects very difficult, if not impossible. Again, while constraints on moving out of classrooms were happily accepted by some, for others they represented a very real conflict with their educational beliefs. One teacher said:

> The chief constraint is the classroom. We've had public edicts here about taking classes outside the classroom, which is a constraint on me. The desks are in rows; there's nothing on the walls: they're remarkably sterile. . . . If I had my way, what I would like to do is take 40 students on a world tour for two years! I took 40-odd away in the holidays and we learned an awful amount. That's what I saw as education.

An extreme case perhaps, but it well illustrates the nature of the conflict.

From another school an experienced teacher said:

> As an English teacher I value most the freedom of choice. Definitely I want freedom of choice of material and the way I would like to use it and the areas I would like to cover. I would not like to have, as we did in the past, one period of this, one period of grammar, one of written expression, one of comprehension. . . . Even my poems and stories were chosen for me. I hated that.

How can such freedoms for the diverse learning priorities of teachers and students—and increasingly of parents—be reconciled with the managerial systems of a big institution? It was clear from our survey that in most schools teachers and students played little part in the framing of the external features of school life, so it was not surprising that the teachers in the survey saw the educational philosophy of the principal as a major element in the context affecting their work. A teacher in a small country high school said about the principal:

> It seems easier to leave school and take trips to expand the students' background mainly because the principal is so very cooperative. . . . He encourages anything we want to try.

The principal himself said:

> I enjoy finding out what teachers are doing, and I enjoy working to make the climate in the school beneficial to everybody. I want my teachers to enjoy teaching; I want my students to enjoy learning and therefore I'll do everything I can to help that.

In a different school two comments by the same teacher point a contrast. She said:

> Yes, we are told here what course we must cover, and we are told, in quite detail, what sections of grammar, what sections of literature, whatever, we must do. We are told what topics we must cover each term, and we are told how the term's marking system will be organized in great detail.

and:

> I don't think I've ever had any writing worth a pinch of salt on anything that's my subject and not the students'. . . . I am finding it very hard to get them to value their own experiences.

Clearly, school administrations and teachers in classrooms have to compromise. It would seem worthwhile to attempt to go beyond the surface of expediency and uncover the nature of the conflicting demands. Then it should be possible for administrators to plan the managerial systems of schools to support rather than constrain the teachers in their purposes.

The Nature of the Conflicting Demands: Multiplicity of Intentions

Each of us teaches—or learns—against a background of intentions, our own and other people's. These are often unrecognized and inexplicit. Teachers are sometimes called boring, and students apathetic; their various intentions have not matched. Take also the fact that teachers of the same subject have diverse personal constructs about it and about education, as do their pupils, and one can begin to see how a multiplicity of intentions is behind the difference in classroom events and classroom climates. Almost no one gets a clear run. The intentionality of school administrations is more difficult to assess. Broadly, they seem to belong to tradition, expediency, and the educational philosophy of the principal and senior staff. Add to these the demands arising from the intentions of parents, and of the generally non-educational purposes of the media, and it is easy to see how school administrations get caught in the crossfire.

Nevertheless, it is now becoming clear that the pursuit of individual intentions is a major element in learning and in teaching. The problem is to find ways of making more of the varying intentions match, or at least accommodate to each other. It is probably true to say that student intentions play little part in most classrooms—except in so far as some students make the teacher's purposes their own; similarly, most staff—other than department heads—have little influence on organizational features which profoundly affect their work. Yet, the managerial system is the means by which the accommodation of diverse intentions could be deliberately planned for, could be built into the institutional framework. There are attempts to do this here and there, but largely the power of intentionality in its widest sense is neither understood nor catered to. The most that most teachers can do at present is to get around the obstructing features in their environments as best they can. Some of their attempts are illustrated in the following examples, which show both the strength of shared learning priorities and the frustrating effects of certain features in the contexts. The final example describes briefly a school whose structure was designed to provide scope for many interactions.

Some Resolutions

The principal of a country high school believed that a school should be an active community institution. He set about creating a community school by extending operations beyond the usual age levels and by involving members of the community in as many aspects of school life as possible. He well understood that institutional features would have to be created to do this. Among these was a school council with standing committees (with student and community representation) for education, finance, grounds and buildings, canteen, agriculture, etc., and the school buildings and resources were available from early morning to late at night. There were many other innovative features, so the school was, as far as it went, an example of a deliberate attempt to create a managerial system which would assist in all sorts of ways the policy of community involvement in the school. It was curious, therefore, to find no set of corresponding features designed to enable the large staff to understand the innovations and to discuss their individual work as part of the broad picture. Department heads and staff engaging in special operations such as Work Experience knew what was afoot, but most staff did not. Meetings were few and never for discussion. The existence of two small staffrooms which had to serve all purposes of a large staff in effect divided teachers into opposing camps; there were no features in the school context that would provide for discussion and resolution of the hostilities. Let's see how the intentions of some of the staff and students fared in this school.

As part of the community school approach, parents were invited to join senior classes to prepare, alongside school students, for qualifying tertiary examinations. The scheme was negotiated in discussion with all parties. The following brief excerpts from interviews with the teachers, the parent-students and the school students seem to show that the intentions of all concerned were known to all and mutually pursued.

INTERVIEWER: (to teachers) Will you tell me something about how the mature students fit into your classes?

TEACHER 1: I find they fit remarkably well. You will see when you come into the class. They're not considered by the others as anything different.

TEACHER 2: And I think it helps them with their own kids. It's amazing the insight one of mine now has just by sitting back and listening to her own boy joining in.

INTERVIEWER: Do you think, perhaps, a case could be made for this happening more generally?

TEACHER 3: I would be all in favor of it. . . . It makes me myself look much more closely at my behavior and my teaching. It opens my eyes. They can see through me far more easily than young students can. . . .

INTERVIEWER: (to mature students) Do you think your presence has had any noticeable effect on the class?

PARENT 1: Well, I think so, because we are quite enthusiastic, and I think that helps, you know.

PARENT 2: You feel nervous the first couple of times but after a while. . . . Everybody is here to learn, and that's the thing about coming to class.

INTERVIEWER: (to school students) Does having mature students in your class make any difference?

JAMES: I see a maturing influence actually. With the mature students in there it seems to keep down a lot of the school romantics. I think we'd probably be a bit rougher and wilder if it wasn't for the mature students.

ROY: They know exactly what they're after—they know what they want to do.

JAMES: I enjoy talking to these people on not necessarily school-related subjects, but it's still quite an education just talking to people. We're rejuvenating them and they're maturing us.

These lessons seemed very successful. Work was serious and enjoyed, and examinations were passed. We noted the following features of the context:

1. Students and teachers worked within the expectations that belong to established examination classes that provided overt purposes.

2. There had been full discussions with staff, students, and parents before the scheme began, and in student and parent councils.

3. The teachers were a small group of experienced staff who were accustomed to discussing and planning their work together; moreover they—observably—agreed about their subject and how to teach it.

4. Discussion of course content and of educational issues were features of the classes; both kinds of students trusted their teachers; the teachers felt free to pursue their own particular interests and styles of teaching within the limits of the examination syllabus.

In effect, these classes and their teachers constituted a well-defined sub-group within the school with specific contexts which supported the intentions of all the participants. The contexts for other English lessons were very different. For instance, a young English teacher working with younger classes in this same school said:

> What I really miss in this school which we had in my other school was all the staff got together in lots of staff meetings. . . . Anybody who had anything they wanted to air could bring it up and it was thrashed out . . . and everything that was going to be innovated the headmaster brought up in front of us and we could argue about it . . . but here I just get the feeling that I'm a sort of teacher who teaches, and things get passed down to me, and that's it.

What began to emerge from this case study and others was, first, the frustration of teachers working in relative isolation, and second, the ways in which teachers created sub-groups in schools where they felt the environment was hostile or indifferent to their educational aims. We found science departments particularly tended to form coherent sub-groups and seemed able to pursue their intentions almost as if they were independent kingdoms. It seemed that it was the existence of the labs as the center of their work that gave them their strength. Labs are a physical center where the work is located, where teachers have their resources, and where they can exchange ideas, plan, and even relax. We observed that science teachers tended to work in isolated groups, and that there was little attempt by school authorities to extrapolate the advantages of science departments into other parts of the school.

Given this lead we looked at English in a school where there was an English staffroom and time set aside for meetings, and compared what went on there with the school described above where there was no English staffroom—only two small general staffrooms.

In the first case the English staffroom had become a center for work in English for teachers and students. Meetings took place there; plans were made and exchanged; conversations took place between lessons; ideas were discussed, both specific to English and more general; students came for consultations and joint meetings. Thus, the level of understanding of mutual intentions was high.

In the other school with only two small general staffrooms, and where classes were peripatetic and there was no center for English, the English department was split down the middle according to divergent views about the subject. Protagonists frequented different staffrooms, and their differing educational aims resulted in two syllabuses for English with two different sets of textbooks. Time and a place to meet were not among the arrangements from the school administration, because they were not perceived as affecting teaching in any significant way. It seemed unlikely that the situation would be improved without some deliberate channel for communication being created.

We found the schools bewildering in the ways in which items in the context of lessons affected what the teachers wanted to do. Senior staff, on the whole, managed to get what they wanted; younger staff suffered most from what appeared to be the random directives of the managerial systems; but one school, from its inception, set out to take account of intentionality at the level of the whole school. In the first instance, this meant the creation of flexible school structures designed to allow teachers to work according to their lights, and secondly to provide for communication between them. Specific concepts of flexible use of space and time and of people determined the physical and psychological features of this school environment for learning. About people the principal said:

> I mentioned about the use of space and time. The third part of the triangle is people. . . . I'm convinced that typically, in a hierarchical, authoritarian structure, good staff members work only at a percentage of their potential—about 70% to 80% perhaps. I feel the environment we have managed to develop here where they're released professionally (as you know, we share decision-making and that kind of thing)—in this kind of environment they explode into action.

"Explode into action"—a powerful image expressing the principal's belief in the power of intentions in learning and teaching. The corollary of this view was a recognition of the need for opportunities for staff and students to communicate with each other. This meant time and places to meet and talk. Both were provided. Every department had a small seminar room close to its teaching area. Lessons were time-tabled with large blocks of time which department heads could juggle with to suit teaching, meetings, or private study. Through their respective councils, students and parents could enter the dialogue.

Thus, in this school, the managerial system was designed to be the means through which many different intentions might be realized. Channels were created through which things could be discussed, and, by agreement, modified. The contexts of work in classrooms were recognized as influential and were designed for support. The central notion of flexibility was an attempt to realize in the structure of an institution the widest scope for the multiplicity of intentions of its members.

It would be a pity if this consideration of some of the contexts for English lessons, and, more generally of learning and teaching in school, were to be interpreted as being of more importance than the imagination and skill of teaching. Enough focus has been given in this paper to the beliefs and attitudes of teachers to suggest that these are the most powerful of all the features in the context of learning; but in school, as in nature, human beings have a habitat which may be favorable or unfavorable and can affect what goes on in lessons, perhaps more than we have realized. Given knowledge of what items in the context most affect what teachers want to do in classrooms, we should be able to develop school structures which support teachers instead of inhibiting them.

Notes and References

[1] Nancy Martin. *What Goes On in English Lessons: Case Studies from Government High Schools in Western Australia.* Education Department, Western Australia, 1980, pp. 1–3.

[2] George A. Kelly. "A Brief Introduction to Personal Construct Theory," in *Perspectives in Personal Construct Theory.* (ed) D. Bannister, Academic Press, New York, 1970.

[3] M. Parlett and D. Hamilton. "Evaluations as Illumination," in *Curriculum Evaluation Today: Trends and Implications.* (ed) D. Tawney, Macmillan Research Series, 1976.

[4] A. Bussis, E. Chittenden and M. Amarel. *Beyond Surface Curriculum: An Interview Study of Teachers' Understanding.* Westview Press, Boulder, Colorado, 1976, pp. 14–18.

13

Genuine Communications:
The Enfranchisement of Young Writers

A Moratorium on Skill-based Writing

There was a secondary school in East London where the English teachers decided to make a concerted effort to teach the use of the apostrophe to show possession. Only this. It wasn't difficult, they thought, and it should be possible to teach this to everyone in the fourth year if all the teachers concentrated on it. They did not succeed. All the writing came in peppered with apostrophes. Some were right, but most were wrong. After that they declared a moratorium. No one was to use apostrophes until enough time had gone by to forget the instructions. Then they would make a fresh and different start.

I want to suggest that we need a moratorium on the very notion of skill as the basis of language development in the mother tongue. True though this notion is—as an aspect of language—and useful though it is in a broad sense, I think the connotations of the term *skills* have come to dominate teaching in a way that is detrimental to learning. To elaborate: We have come to think of the process of writing as consisting of isolable elements which can be taught separately. We have used analogies which have seemed useful, such as practicing piano scales or strokes in tennis which—for whatever reasons—have led us astray in teaching language. The writing assignments given to students have been—and are still, I would say—dominated by the idea of "practice"—for some future, unspecified use.

Yet, language exists in a context of immediate use, exists to do something with *now* and is therefore rooted in a context of meaning. Moreover, children come to school having already learned the system through learn-

Adapted from *Topics in Learning & Learning Disabilities* 3:3, by permission of Aspen Systems Corporation © 1983.

ing to speak, so it is already a going concern for them. It is true they now have to master the written language (reading and writing) and I think this is where the trouble with skills and practice has set in. There is a widespread notion that errors reinforce themselves, so they need to be corrected as they occur. This puts the focus on formal aspects of writing instead of on its purpose. Language is after all essentially pragmatic in real life. We make it work in rough and ready ways. So the question we could more properly ask instead of "Is it right?" would be "Did it work?"

In early learning of any kind, errors are accepted as an inevitable part of the effort to do something, or say something. They are part of the process of learning, as Bruner's observations of the reciprocity of effort and interpretation between mothers and infants show. In this context of reciprocal engagement it is illuminating to look at two instances as illustrations of points on a kind of learning scale. Rachel at one-and-a-half years engages in bursts of utterance, not words in any recognizable sense, though occasionally a recognizable word occurs like "Ted" (her teddy bear); but they have all the recognizable intonations of a conversational utterance expecting a response. And the adult replies as best as she can, guessing at meaning and thus maintaining the sound pattern of the "conversation." The engagement is similar to that described by Bruner. Notions of error are nowhere on the horizon. There is only pleasure and response.

Then jump five years and consider Antony, aged 6. He is at school and has learned to write. Out of his new mastery he writes stories at home for his mother where there is continuity with his earlier pre-school language learning—pleasure in what he writes and acceptance of his experiments with the written language. At school the situation is radically different. His mother had asked him why he didn't write longer stories for his teacher when he wrote such good stories for her. His reply epitomized the effects of a skills approach to early writing. He said, "I don't like writing stories at school. I'm frightened of getting mistakes. I don't know how to spell some words and I forget full stops." Examples of his stories written in the two fundamentally different contexts illustrates the destructive nature of the school context.

Here are two of the many short pieces he wrote at school. All were of similar length and pattern:

1. I like the rocks. In the water there are fish. I catch them. I have got a fish now.
2. I have a draw. I have a treasure. It is in my cupboard. I take it out sometimes.

Note the short sentences and the absence of any connections which could raise the problem of punctuation. A high-risk situation which he met by writing as little as possible. In contrast, here is one of the stories he wrote at home for his mother.

The bird that flew across the sea.

One day I saw a bird. I chast it. It flew over the sea. I watched it. It flew fast and dropped some fethers and then flew away again. I stac at it. I got a little canoe and I started to row. I folode it everywhere. I would not lose it. I went so fast the boat nearly tipped but i didn't because I pulled the orws to fast. I saw a big ship. I got in it. I asked the kapten to go faster and faster so he did. I cept watching it. I would not take my eyes off it. The bird flew on. the ship went so fast the people were scad so I said to the kapten go faster and faster. I said to the people do not be scad. I lost the bird.

Note the length, the range of words and syntax and the sense of story form. But we may surmise that from this point on till the end of schooling, unless he is lucky, Antony will remain convinced that his teachers are not interested in what he has to say, but only in how he says it, so the most crucial element in his growth as a writer has been taken from him—the interested reader who will take up the dialogue of his *ideas.* Writing has thus become an exercise, a dummy run. The disabling process has been well and truly set in motion.

There are, of course, other kinds and causes of disability, but this one is the most general and the most widespread in its effects.

Genuine Communication

For skills and the drills that go with them we need to substitute the notion of "genuine communication." Genuine communication for children in whatever context—writing for history, English, science, a letter, a diary, or their usually informative special interests—is very often going to mean an inseparable blend of giving an account of the topic and expressing their feelings about it. If this is so, we should accept the mixture; if we discourage the personal element in it, we risk making writing an unwieldy and alien instrument instead of a natural extension of the children's own mental process. And accepting it means more than simply allowing it to happen: it means agreeing to be communicated with in this way and making ourselves a real audience by giving an authentic response to the communication as a communication rather than by giving back an evaluation of how well the writing has been accomplished.

The London University Model

The London University writing research unit under the leadership of James Britton called this kind of writing "expressive." We characterized it as the kind of writing which reflects the ebb and flow of a writer's thoughts and feelings and takes for granted that the writers themselves are of interest to the reader, so expressions of attitude are an integral part of this kind of writing. It is often relatively unstructured and assumes a reader willing to take the unexpressed on trust.

We were working on a model which would allow us to characterize all school writing. We set out to answer two questions: "What is the writing for?" and "Who is it for?" In looking at some 2000 scripts to try to answer these questions we produced a two-dimensional model of Function and Audience as being the major factors affecting writing. In our Function model we saw expressive writing as a kind of matrix from which writers moved in one of two opposite directions: either towards what we called "transactional" writing or towards "poetic" writing.

Transactional writing, often called "expository," is concerned with some direct result or transaction such as giving information, presenting an argument or a literary judgment, or writing reports, essays, notes, etc. It is the language of science, commerce, and technology and it is taken for granted that the writer can be challenged for truthfulness to public knowledge and logicality. The major part of all school writing at the secondary level is of this kind.

Poetic writing on the other hand is without any such *direct* practical purpose, and includes stories, poems, and plays. It is taken for granted that true or false is not a relevant question at the literal level and since there is no transaction afoot, its reader is free to attend to the formal features—patterns of events or sounds or emotions, these being an integral part of the meaning.

Our "Sense of Audience" model identified the various audiences that the school writings seemed to be directed towards. These covered the self (private journals and notes, for example), peer groups, the teacher in a number of very different roles—trusted adult or partner in a dialogue or the teacher as assessor and examiner. Finally there was the writer to his reader (general public). The bulk of the writings in our sample were for teachers as examiners (judges of rightness or wrongness). Expressive writing, of course, assumed an audience of either the teacher in the role of trusted adult or of a peer group.

The Usefulness of the Model in Looking at Language Development

The two models of Function and A Sense of Audience make it possible to look at the range of writing which students are doing in all their school work, and it allows us to be quite precise about the development of their ability to write appropriately for different purposes and different audiences.

Development is to a large extent a process of specialization and differentiation. We start by writing the way we talk to each other—expressively and envisaging our reader as a single, real, known person; gradually we may acquire, in addition, the capacity to use transactional and poetic writing, and to write for an unspecified generalized or unknown audience. The development of writing abilities is partly conditional on the more general development of students out of egocentrism. Writing itself can aid that general development, but if we want it to be a means of thinking and active organizing, the writer must feel he is making a genuine communication and not just performing an exercise—which was how David, aged 13, saw it: "You write it down just to show the teacher that you've done it, but it doesn't bring out any more knowledge in you."

Young Writers Need Their Own Topics

Young writers need their own topics as well as their own language; otherwise there isn't much chance of a genuine communication. Donald Graves and his associates at the New Hampshire Writing Process Laboratory have done much work in recent years with beginning writers. First and foremost they choose their own topics. Donald Graves says, "When children do the pushing, they have control. Child control is defined in this study as child initiative. Children choose their topics, language inventions, discover space on the paper; teachers follow, observing, solving problems with them, in order to steer their craft into greater clarity."

Again, Lucy McCormick Calkins writing about Atkinson Elementary School in rural New Hampshire says, "Teachers at Atkinson insist that writers choose their own topics. Their reasons are:

1. Deciding what you have to say is probably the hardest and most important part of writing. We cannot take this responsibility away from the writer.
2. As children consider, select and reconsider their topics, they experience the revision process. This is often the first and easiest form of revision.
3. When writers write what they know and care about, their writing is their own; they are driven to make it good. They supply the initiative and the motivation."

The Problem in Secondary Schools: Book Knowledge and the Language That It Comes In

Many elementary teachers have gone a long way towards enfranchising young writers, by freedom of topic, by accepting their personal, expressive language, and by shifting their own role from assessor and corrector to that of interested reader and adviser in revisions. The situation in secondary schools is very different. Since most high schools are organized on a subject basis, students write for a number of different teachers in their different subjects. Almost all the writing is transactional, and the generally held view is that the required writing is formal and impersonal as for an unknown public audience. Most teachers set the topics and most writing is graded. By producing the kind of writing their teachers seem to want, students hope to gain a good mark. Over the years they lose the six-year-old's sense of having things to say of their own. Meanwhile teachers suppose that students cannot write without suggested topics and the incentive of marks—and indeed, unless the context is changed, they cannot. As a College of Education student wrote, "At secondary school it was always writing to please whichever teacher was teaching you."

There is, of course, a real problem with transactional writing in high school. It is the problem of book knowledge; how to deal with it, how to assimilate it and how to mold it into writing. Most students find both the book knowledge and the language it comes in difficult. A student said:

> I know what he was on about, but I only know what he was on about in my words. I didn't know his words. In my exams I had to change the way I learnt, you know. In all my exercise books, I put it down the way I understood, but I had to remember what I had written there and then translate it into what I think *they* will understand.

In the five-year project, *Writing Across the Curriculum,* we set out to track down classrooms where the majority of the students—not just the exceptional ones—succeeded in assimilating book knowledge and writing about it well while remaining at the center of their own learning, as it were. We wanted to know what the classroom conditions might be where this happened, what the setting was—how the teachers worked with the students.

Our findings were illuminating and had clear links with the changed procedures in elementary schools described above. We were looking particularly at students in their sixteenth or examination year where there is a heavy premium on the recapitulation of book knowledge.

The educational settings of those classes when the students were making sense for themselves of their new knowledge and yet operating in a good transactional mode had the following features:

1. The writing started from firsthand experience.
2. The assignments were long-term studies, not essay-type exam answers.
3. There was individual choice of topics (within the general subject field—in these cases Social or Community Studies). Some examples were: working with physically handicapped people, play schools, alternative societies, the re-housing of my grandparents, the redevelopment of one of the oldest bits of our city.

4. All kept work journals which they were expected to draw on in writing up their study.
5. The firsthand experience in these studies was extended by secondary experience of different kinds. Different students made different use of secondary sources, some going chiefly to books for their information, others relying more on what they learned from other people.
6. These conditions were the result of agreed aims and practices by teachers concerned.
7. The teachers came into the picture of this writing as advisers and trusted critics. They helped students settle on their topic, advised them where to go for sources, and how to organize and present their work, including constructing questionnaires, drawing on their journals, using quotations from interviews and books. In the introduction, the students reflected on the work they had been doing and assessed its value to them, thus demonstrating some kind of perspective for their learning.

All the studies were competent and interesting, though not all had mastered the traditional forms of transactional writing, but it seemed to us that in our search for good transactional writing we had stumbled on something much bigger. The context of these studies had altered the *learning* process for these students. They were on the way to becoming autonomous learners (not passive recipients). The crucial change in the role of the teachers (partners rather than directors) cleared the way for the students' own intentions. Furthermore, the variety of language forms available from journals, interviews, and books set the students on the road to finding an appropriate language of their own; the best wrote admirably while the least able were on the edge of escape from the all-pervading school sense that you must use other people's language, the language you may never manage.

Unfortunately, this is not the whole story. One has to ask how these students would fare in other subjects where teachers were likely to make more traditional demands on their writing. One can only say that students are pretty adaptable with regard to the idiosyncrasies of their various teachers, and if they do over a period of time experience the satisfactions of writing and learning and have the opportunity to reflect on this linked process, it may enable them to take other demands in their stride, though a more explicit policy by teachers can help students to perceive that there are many different purposes for writing. For instance, an English chemistry teacher taught her classes to write up their science experiments in the traditional manner, but she also asked them to write their own journals of work in science lessons. These were not marked but were always read and spoken about. It seemed that the brief and stylized work of science reports did not satisfy the students. They felt a need to use more involved and expressive language and to comment on work that had interested them. For instance, one young student wrote:

> Today we did some experiments following on last weeks. There were some good ones this week. One was iodine. There was only a tiny bit of it in the test tube. When it was heated it made a deep mauve vapour up the tube with a glitter on the sides of the test tube. When it was cool the deep mauve vapour disappears and only the glitter was left. Another good one was Ammonium Dichromate. It started as orange granules, but when heated it sparked, bubbled and began to blow out of the tube. . . . There were some other things that we done today but they were not as good.

Experience is not truly our own until it has been articulated in our own language, yet in most subjects in high schools there is little opportunity for students to use their own language about their new learning or to reflect on it.

Primary Trait Scoring Puts Expressive Writing on the Map

Very recently James D. Atwater wrote a report to the Ford Foundation called *Better Testing, Better Writing*. This report was a critique of a study published by the Central Midwestern Regional Education Laboratory (CEMREL). The study was designed to be a guide to the Primary Trait Scoring System (P.T.S.), applied in this case to teaching, not testing. Atwater said about the study, "Simply as a testing tool, one that evaluates a child's ability to write on a systematic basis, P.T.S. is already a success. But what caught my interest was the next giant step: using P.T.S. not just to test, but to teach." Of course, P.T.S. may be used to score grammar, spelling, and other important mechanics of composition, but the breakthrough in this case comes, I believe, because the CEMREL team used *kinds of discourse* rather than stylistic features as their primary traits for scoring; the kinds of discourse they settled on were transactional, persuasive, expressive, but their initial study was of expressive writing. They say, "Expressive writing enables children to make sense for themselves of what they have seen or read or done or talked about by composing it for themselves in their own words. Thus expressive writing is fundamental to learning—in any subject matter—because it enables children to internalize knowledge, to make it part of themselves, by putting it together in their own terms." Thus, the study is a breakthrough on two fronts: the perception of kinds of discourse as primary traits, and the recognition of personal experience as the prime mover in writing. The title of the CEMREL publication says it all: *An Experimental Guide to the Primary Trait System, Composing Childhood Experience: An Approach to Writing and Learning in the Elementary Grades.*

No one hitherto has worked on criteria for assessing expressive writing, or on systematic leads into other modes of discourse. Don Miller and his colleagues at CEMREL did just this. They say, "The primary trait, or purpose, of the exercise is the inventive elaboration of a role through the writer revealing personal feeling and ideas." Their criteria for defining the score categories were:

1. Entry into the role
2. Elaboration of the role
3. Expression of feeling within the role.

However, they observe that whereas assessment is the primary goal of N.A.E.P. (National Assessment of Educational Progress), it is of secondary importance in the classroom, where P.T.S. is a means to an end, not an end in itself. The end is improved writing and learning. Thus P.T.S. becomes a kind of structural aid to teachers, to be used in conjunction with other ideas and practices that have been developed as aspects of teaching writing—for instance, relevant discussion in groups or, with the teacher, the sharing of drafts, discussion of roles, etc. And within this general framework of pre-writing, writing and rewriting, the children move through writing which takes up imagined roles in situations to role-playing narratives and story writing to personal experience with comment which leads out of narrative into explanation, or personalized (expressive) thinking and writing about more abstract matters.

In his critique of *Composing Childhood Experience* Atwater comments that the scoring aspects of P.T.S. have to be handled very carefully, but he believes its advantages far outweigh the disadvantages since public pressures to show students' progress in writing are likely to tempt school administrators to fall back on testing easily measurable things—spelling, grammar, and capitalization—rather than written discourse as a coherent and purposive composition. I would comment here that one can cut one's throat with a carving knife as well as cut the meat, and it is primary trait scoring *underpinned* by a theoretical understanding of the relation of writing to learning which gives the CEMREL study its dimensions.

Who Benefits Most from the Freedom to Use Expressive Writing?

Expressive writing is appropriate for first drafts and therefore offers enfranchisement—though able students may get by somehow without it—to all writers, but it is crucial for beginning writers and slow learners. They are crippled if they cannot use it, crippled in their learning and crippled in their writing. Peter Medway, a British writer, likens the struggle to gain acceptance for personal forms of writing to the demands that the Bible be printed in English, not in Latin, and that people be allowed to discuss it and interpret it for themselves. He says:

> The "linguistic deprivation" to be taken seriously is the one for which we ourselves are responsible, since denial of the right to talk and write in personal modes is a reduction of the chance to learn. It is in effect a human rights issue.

Of course, this does not mean that other kinds of writing are not important, and I have suggested above that progress in writing may be defined as the capacity to move about in the kinds of language appropriate for different purposes and audiences, but I am suggesting that without recourse to their own language many children will never willingly write much more than their own names.

Journals

While first drafts of any writing may be expressive, the final form of expository writing for a public audience (or critical/explanatory essays) would not be appropriate in expressive writing, whereas journals of all sorts are by their very nature appropriate. They have no recognizable form; they reflect any aspect of the writer's life, thought and feeling; they range from the trivial to the abstract. In schools they can be located in a particular field of study and be re-named "work journal" or "learning log." A caveat is however necessary. They should not become just another school exercise to be graded and corrected. If this happens their function will change and their effectiveness as a vehicle for expressive writing will vanish. As Peter Medway says, this is because "expressive student language—a personal and revealing language of wondering, questioning, tentative formulation and risk-taking comment—is not available to order. It *may* occur when two conditions are met—when the writers are interested in the subject, and feel at ease with their audiences—but it takes two to make the necessary relationship of trust and security." Grading will destroy this.

However, even when journals are ungraded and elicit some written reply from the teacher, there remains the problem of what a British science teacher called "mainstream" writing. He says:

> There were some interesting pieces (in journals) produced by kids with learning difficulties like Lisa whose work was often very short and if she did write at length whole sections were incomprehensible with missing information and breakdowns in syntax. Her journal entries improved in length, fluency and accuracy, but this progress was not transferred to her "mainstream" writing. Similarly, Adrian, an-

other student with learning difficulties wrote the following in his journal—a real breakthrough for him:

Fishing

When I go fishing next I would like to catch a big pike, 14 lbs in weight. And take it home to show my mum and dad and my sister. Then I would skin it then cook it and eat it. I have never caught anything and even if I catch a small fish I will be pleased with myself.

But Adrian, like Lisa, was not able to transfer this quality to his mainstream writing.

Language Across the Curriculum: Language Policies for Schools

The only solution to this problem of the kinds of writing demands made by subject teachers in high schools would seem to be discussion among staff members of the place of language in all learning, and agreement by at least some staff to encourage a variety of forms. For instance, "learning logs" in addition to the traditional forms of expository writing could be part of all subject teachers' work in their own subjects. A British physics teacher of senior students wrote:

> I am hoping that responding to their entries in a helpful, informative and conversational way will instigate further dialogue between us about the learning processes needed for the work that my students undertake in physics lessons . . . they may develop in other directions which at present I know nothing about. It is this "not knowing" which makes learning logs and their possibilities a new and exciting adventure.

This teacher from perhaps the toughest of all school subjects also said, "There are many questions that probably arise in anyone's mind before they decide to try out learning logs with a class. These are some that went through mine: Will I be laughed at by other members of staff? Will it be worthwhile to spend valuable time on the logs? Will the students see the point or will they resent all this 'extra writing'?" The answers to these questions can only come from discussion among the staff and trials by those convinced enough to experiment. Such experiments and such discussion are at the heart of what is meant by "language across the curriculum."

The Alternative Mode: Stories, Poems, and Plays

While expressive writing is beginning to come into its own as a major instrument of learning, the symbolic transformation of experience which James Moffett calls "the mythic mode," i.e. stories, poems and plays, is broadly speaking, seen only in its most influential form as literature—a different study from school writing. Yet, school students have been familiar with its forms since their earliest days, and their stories, however primitive, are of the same genre. I want to suggest that we largely underestimate the compelling power of what the London Writing Research team called "poetic" writing. James Britton says

> It takes a Vygotsky, speaking across the decades since his death, to observe that the attempt to teach writing as a motor skill is mistaken . . . it was his view that make-believe play, drawing and writing should be seen as "different moments in an essentially unified process of development of written language" . . . since pictorial representation is first-order symbolism and writing is second-order symbolism, Vygotsky saw this discovery as a key point in the development of writing in a child.

In the stories that children tell or write—as in make-believe play—they remake their lives, inextricably mingled with the stories they have encountered, yet this powerful (and familiar) reconstructive process is largely unrecognized in its significance in the learning and writing process. Certainly in high schools it is not recognized as an alternative mode of great potential for synthesizing learning and interpreting it. One of the virtues of the "formlessness" of journals is that students can be encouraged to include poems or stories in them, and many have done this when they felt a need for the anonymity given by story form. In such symbolic transformations they can try out roles and present views they may not be willing to do directly.

We also underestimate the somewhat mysterious power of story writing, which provides a drive which just is not there in transactional writing, a drive which gives greater length and fluency to slow learners and which carries them over some of the language barriers. With inexperienced writers or slow learners, stories and poems are forms of expressive writing, often a long way from the more complete shaping of true poetic writing. But the power of story writing, together with the freedom to use their own personal language, is likely to give slow learners their best access to writing. Moreover, since stories are about the possible rather than the actual, they give young writers access to the *hypothetical* modes, i.e. they can see their own experience as something that can be improvised on. Language frees them from actuality. If story writing could be recognized as a mode which synthesizes experiences, preoccupations and emotions rather than as fanciful fictions, it could become as important in the development of writers as expressive writing is becoming.

Two Practical Matters

Two Processes, Not One

In a recent book Frank Smith describes the activities of two people jointly engaged in writing. The author is engaged in getting ideas, uttering them as they come and doing some selecting of words and phrases as he goes. The other, a secretary perhaps, has the physical effort of writing, and is concerned with spelling, capitalization, punctuation, paragraphs and legibility. By the simple device of describing the two processes—composing and transcribing as being undertaken by two people—Frank Smith has highlighted the dual process, which in schools is usually seen as one process. No wonder students fall between the two. They are two processes and need to be separated and worked on at different times.

Extended Talk

Students with writing difficulties can be helped in their learning by having the opportunity to utter into a tape-recorder whatever they might otherwise have written. Many are able to do this quite competently and the extended talk helps them to organize and internalize their learning in the same way that writing does, especially if they listen to a playback with their teacher. There is much more group talk in schools than there used to be, but little opportunity for extended talk by students, and for those who write little and with difficulty, extended talk can be a valuable addition to their language repertoire.

References

James Atwater. *Better Testing, Better Writing.* A Report to the Ford Foundation, 1981.

James Britton. "Spectator Role and the Beginning of Writing," in *What Writers Know: The Language Process and the Structure of Written Discourse.* Academic Press, 1982.

James Britton, Anthony Burgess, Nancy Martin, Alex McLeod and Harold Rosen. *The Development of Writing Abilities 11–18.* Macmillan Research Series, 1975.

Jerome Bruner. From lectures delivered in 1977 and 1978 as Professor of Psychology at Oxford.

Lucy McCormick Calkins. "Writing Taps a New Source of Energy," in *Principal Magazine,* 1980.

Kevin Eames. *Whatever Comes to Mind: An Experiment in Journal Writing.* Booklet No. 3, Learning about Learning, Wiltshire Education Authority, 1981.

Donald Graves. "Let the Children Show Us How to Write," in *Visible Language,* Vol. 3, no. 1, March 1979.

Greg Jones. "Experimenting with Learning Logs in Physics," in *Learning to Think in Science Lessons,* Booklet No. 6 in Learning about Learning, Wiltshire Education Authority, 1981.

Carl Klaus, Richard Lloyd-Jones, Don Miller et al. *An Experimental Guide to the Primary Trait System, Composing Childhood Experience: An Approach to Writing and Learning in the Elementary Grades.* CEMREL, Inc., 1979.

Nancy Martin, Pat D'Arcy, Bryan Newton and Robert Parker. *Writing and Learning Across the Curriculum 11–16.* Ward Lock, 1976.

Peter Medway. "The Bible and the Vernacular: The Significance of Language Across the Curriculum," in *English in Education,* Vol. 15, No. 1, Spring 1981.

James Moffett. *Teaching the Universe of Discourse.* Houghton Mifflin, 1968.

Frank Smith. *Writing and the Writer.* Holt, Rinehart and Winston, 1982.

Lev Vygotsky. "The Pre-history of Written Language," in *Mind and Society.* Harvard University Press, 1978.